CONTRADICTION PHILOSOPHY

RAMAKRISHNA CHEBOLI

INDIA • SINGAPORE • MALAYSIA

ISBN 979-8-89026-015-4

Dedicated to the Oblation

THIS BOOK WAS WRITTEN IN INDIA DURING
2020-2022

CONTENTS

PREFACE *13*

I
STATE OF MIND

1. EQUANIMOUS 16
2. CONTRADICTION 17
3. UNDERSTANDING 18
4. SPECULATION 19
5. MATERIALIST 20
6. SPIRITUAL 21
7. PROPORTION 22
8. SCINETIFIC 23
9. ASTRONOMICAL 24
10. ASTROLOGICAL 25
11. INTELLECT 26
12. DUALITY 27
13. SUPREME 28
14. ADVAITA 29
15. DVAITA 30
16. KALIYUGA 31
17. KALKI 32
18. PRALAYA 33
19. PRIORITIES 34

20. LUCIFER ... 35
21. TRAIN ... 36
22. ALIVE ... 37
23. DEAD ... 38
24. TRANSCENDED ... 39
25. GROUNDED ... 40
26. SPECIES ... 41
27. PERSONAGE ... 42
28. TATTVABODHA ... 43
29. DRIK AND DRISHYA ... 44
30. BRAHMA SUTRA ... 45
31. CONTEMPORARY ... 46
32. OMEN ... 47
33. STORY ... 48
34. PAPA ... 49
35. PUNYA ... 50
36. BANDHAN ... 51
37. PURNAM ... 52
38. NATURE ... 53
39. PROGRESSION OF TIME ... 54
40. UNDERSTANDING ... 55
41. MANAS ... 56
42. CONTENTION ... 57
43. STAGE ... 58
44. SPECULATION ... 59
45. UNSCIENTIFIC ... 60
46. DEVI ... 61
47. ELEMENTS ... 62
48. CHANT ... 63
49. KAMA ... 64

50. MEDHA . . . 65
51. OBLATION . . . 66
52. NEURONS . . . 67
53. WORDS . . . 68
54. WITHIN . . . 69
55. LOGIC . . . 70
56. THINK . . . 71
57. SRI . . . 72
58. LAKSHMI . . . 73
59. PURUSHA . . . 74
60. RITUAL . . . 75
61. INVOLVEMENT . . . 76
62. DURGA . . . 77
63. PERSPECTIVE . . . 78
64. SPOKEN . . . 79
65. DISASTER . . . 80
66. DREAM . . . 81
67. NARAYANA . . . 82
68. RUDRA . . . 83
69. SUPREME . . . 84
70. VISHNU . . . 85
71. TRINITY . . . 86
72. DELUSION . . . 87
73. SKY AND EARTH . . . 88
74. COMMUNICATION . . . 89
75. BLISS . . . 90
76. RESPECT . . . 91
77. FREEDOM . . . 92
78. EVOLUTION . . . 93
79. SUBLIME . . . 94

II
STATE OF THE ART

80. METAPHYSICAL ... 96
81. ABSTRACT ... 97
82. LIFE ... 98
83. SIMPLICITY ... 99
84. PARTICLES ... 100
85. CIVILIZATION ... 101
86. VEDA ... 102
87. SPECULATIVE PHILOSOPHY ... 103
88. EXEMPLIFICATION ... 104
89. SUBJECTIVITY ... 105
90. SCIENCE AND TECHNOLOGY ... 106
91. LOGIC ... 107
92. MACHINE ... 108
93. EXPERIENTIALISM ... 109
94. MANAGEMENT STRUCTURES ... 110
95. PRECEDENCE ... 111
96. EXTRATERRESTRIAL AND BEYOND ... 112
97. DUALITY ... 113
98. BEGINNING AND ENDING ... 114
99. STATE OF THE ART ... 115
100. MIND SPACE AND HUMAN MIND ... 116
101. TIME ... 117
102. SWADHARMA AND NORMATIVENESS ... 118
103. EXISTENT AND NON-EXISTENT ... 119
104. INCORRECTNESS ... 120
105. INCOMPLETENESS ... 121
106. DISCONNECTS ... 122
107. STORY ... 123

108. FAILURES AND CYNICISM 124
109. PURPOSE OF LIFE AND CELEBRATIVENESS 125
110. EXCLUSIVITIES AND SOCIAL ORGANIZATIONS.... 126
111. PSYCHOLOGY AND BOMBS 127
112. GOD 128
113. SPACE 129
114. PARALLELISM 130
115. DIFFICULTY AND MEMORY....................... 131
116. INDEPENDENT RESEARCH 132
117. LANGUAGE AND COMMUNICATION 133
118. MEDITATION AND SILENCE 134
119. ECONOMIC SYSTEM 135
120. CRITICISM 136
121. OPINIONS.................................... 137
122. REAL AND REALISM 138
123. BEAUTY AND BHAKTI........................... 139
124. SOCIAL SERVICE.............................. 140
125. AKARMA...................................... 141
126. DOUBTS AND MISTAKES 142
127. EVERYTHING AND ANYTHING..................... 143
128. CREATIONISM................................. 144
129. AGREEMENTS AND DISAGREEMENTS 145
130. UNDERSTANDING AND UNUNDESRSTANDING.... 146
131. VOLITION AND FREEDOM........................ 147
132. NECROMANCY 148
133. CORRECTNESS, INCORRECTNESS AND RESPECT .. 149
134. CONFIGURATIONS.............................. 150
135. PROOF OF BEING AND ETERNAL.................. 151
136. CONNECTS AND DISCONNECTS.................... 152
137. MANIFEST AND UNMANIFEST..................... 153
138. ANALYSIS 154

139. OPTIONS AND EXERCISE 155
140. INFINITY AND ABSOLUTE 156
141. OPPORTUNITY AND DETERRENT 157
142. ACTUALITIES AND PERSONIFICATION.......................... 158
143. SIMILARITIES AND DIFFERENCES.......................... 159
144. SELF AND MUSIC 160
145. REPETITION AND SYSTEM 161
146. CIVILIZATIONAL BASELINES.......................... 162
147. MORALITIES AND IMPOSSIBILITIES.......................... 163
148. BLANDNESS AND PLANNEDNESS 164
149. LIKES AND DISLIKES.......................... 165
150. SENSITIVITY AND SENSES.......................... 166
151. SEQUENTIALLY.......................... 167
152. EFFECTUALITY 168
153. LEARNING AND UNLEARNING.......................... 169
154. MENTAL DISPOSITIONS.......................... 170
155. ALGORITHMS 171
156. CONVERGENCE AND CONCLUSIVITY.......................... 172
157. MIRRORS 173
158. RITAM.......................... 174
159. PRECLUSIVE.......................... 175
160. PRESENT.......................... 176
161. ANALYSIS 177
162. ATTIRE 178
163. ABUNDANCE 179
164. OBJECTIVITY.......................... 181
165. QUAINTNESS.......................... 183
166. VISIBILITY 184
167. LOVE 185
168. NATURE 187
169. COHESION 188

III
STATE OF TODAY

170. GOVERNENCE 190
171. EVOLUTION 192
172. SUCCESS 194
173. SOCIAL 196
174. RELEVANCE OF HUMAN PARTICIPATION 198
175. INCOMPLETENESS 200
176. ANTHROPOLOGY AND RELIGION 202
177. PURPOSE 204
178. SPACE 206
179. NEGATION 208
180. HISTORY 210
181. IMPORTANCE OF MINDFUL CREATION 212
182. POPULAR BELIEFS 214
183. LANGUAGE 216
184. NUANCE 218
185. REDUNDANT EXPRESSIONS 220
186. CIRCULAR CONSTRUCTS 222
187. SELF ABNEGATION 224
188. COMMUNICATIONS 226
189. EGO AND IMPOSED STORY 228
190. USE OF DREAMS 230
191. SOCIAL SENTIMENT 232
192. MANAGEMENT 234
193. MEDIA 236
194. STORY OF SIMPLICITY 238
195. SCHOOLS 240
196. ESTABLISHMENT 242

197. HUMAN.......................................244
198. INCENTIVES..................................246
199. ADHERENCE...................................248
200. FAILURES....................................250

PREFACE

Belief is the heart of the universe. But there is no quantification that tells you to explain yourself. The only thing that does not need your identity is the mindful. So if I do not ask for an explanation, what is consistent to what you need to understand to explain and to what. Nevertheless, the most controversial in this world is to justify ones statement. The ramifications of diverse thought that may be supportive is just a matter of creative dream works. Dream is also the nature of the sublime. So how does the materialistic version of its supportive argument gets construed. It is only the way people become is the difference. How does one qualify a human from the other.

Direct interactions among humans is not necessary to elucidate. Everything in this world is saturated to a point where we just have all the stories narrated and we just say yes or no to what we think is correct. So when this extravagant communication of explain the world to you for free syndrome happened. The probability of dream being supportive of religion is understood, but a dream being politically subversive to uphold a misfaith is not found yet. So my attempt is to spoil the simplistic and into complication so only a human can understand and the inhuman fails to see the business perspective of what I propose.

I believe there exist contradictions in the mind. This is often the heart of the intellectual. But, arguing relentlessly is the art of the subversive. The point is, that, it is often very difficult to understand life and Nature and God as to where we are going with our harmony. The more difficult is where are the digressed finding even the time and space to even argue their solidarity. With all jurisdiction I have followed the faith of complicating things for you and me. A human still has a chance to understand the complication but the other kind will have to drive their speculative time machines to understand how to live life and understand with un instinctive nature of the eternal bliss.

I

STATE OF MIND

1

EQUANIMOUS

I have an opinion on the things, so my mind is poised. Life gets reviewed based on how one has been. And it is reflected in a seemingly a thought process. What is observing us is a dream and what is contending us is a dream. So we are dream chasers to the best of our intellect. If we get a bit more sophisticated we let the dream chase itself and be proud. The sense I proclaim here is still relativistic. I have thought more on the subject but the expression is in a similar language. So forgive the possibility of the equality to have prevailed all across bringing all of the continuum into the same place.

2

CONTRADICTION

The few signs why I have been different from you is not evident. Sometimes we contradict. And the more we see the two sides of the story the more we become atheist, not so literally. The arguments on both sides occur to us. We need to contain both of them in the safe hands of the credulity of not having understood it completely. Let us me understand the constrain of being thoughtful and also aware not to think some one else's mind. The works of the existence are too personal even if we tried to inflict. The passion is the world that serves the madness of the instinct, we have to believe in our own story.

3

UNDERSTANDING

Basically the problem is we can understand things if put together in a short story and narrated to us like one real life led its way into the mirage. Every one and every thing is real. So looking at some one else's mind is the realistic feeling we have, such a empathy we all hold. But the point of discerning is what is different among us that ones reality is just a dream for the other. So, in spite of the conglomerate of the communist fathoming we haven't focused on the real problems so lets be unanimous is quite the time spent on being equal to one another. I am not racist, but the stories of the order put into place will not be applicable to us as we think.

4

SPECULATION

There always has been the contention who will criticize the methods of democracy for example. The old fangled theory of equation that is pertinent to you and me has either existed all along or we are too disparate subjects different enough not to argue why not to look into the democracy as an alternative to religion. So how to mitigate the misinterpretation of social value and the friends we have in the language of the democratic is to see how the opportunist is using a political argument. We all have to speculate how we present our life tomorrow, if it appears in the public media.

5

MATERIALIST

Life time of a human imposes several restrictions on the politics. Most political not to represent human life of being responsible is Democracy. On the other hand if we control the humans to being responsible of the story being committed in the social it is the dictatorial prowess not to allow the wayward story of human saga to being the social psychology. The capitalist has wielded the weapon without telling entire truth about itself to all of us and the socialist has generalized the arguments as being the same for you and me.

6

SPIRITUAL

The condition, one of which usually happened when we lose the physical contact is called spirituality. In this context, because we override the instinct of being materialistic in our own whimsical nature, it proposes the involvement of the responsibility we have not fathomed while we were being clever while living our life. Spiritual existence is the real part that never lies. We are all accountable to our soul no matter what we do, it has the connection with the natural law. So the jurisdiction often happens when we are done with a life time of drama.

7

PROPORTION

The materialistic life is not what you think it is. What it suggests is that because of the spectrum of the things are being orchestrated around us we also need to be multifaceted. We need to proportion our prowess and the energies into all the things that need equal attention. Stereotypical heroes do happen but it is difficult to save them from their romantic conclusion. So we need to ascertain we are looking into the diversified model of the world. There are ten equations we need to solve in a day and every one takes an hour of our attention.

8

SCINETIFIC

Lets start the argument here. Is it religion or is it scientific the universe is. Primordial argument that has been for ever. The split in just being argumentative which side we are on has depleted the intellect from this argument completely. Science believed in atoms while the religion believes in a dream. So not to commit to a woman too easily we need to evolve a decision based on our intellect. To most part, the religion is correct because it is all a dream. But existentially we are in a world which requires materialistic outlook. So argue the atoms and be opportunistic.

9

ASTRONOMICAL

There is the Sun the source of all energy that prevails in this place. The energy regained from the Sun created and sustained all the based evolution of atomic and molecular nature. the stars are of similar character. Giving us energy to thrive. And there is the hydrogen bomb that works similar to a star. So what is that a star gives us and what destruction it may create is our conceptualization. The religion presents an alternative to reason of astronomical objects as having a human like instinct. So how do we convert astronomy into astrology is a long story.

10

ASTROLOGICAL

The basic precept of religion is not to treat everything as atoms and molecules. It places the argument that everything has a life associated with itself and a consciousness to thrive. Each entity we see has a lifetime of sense and character of its own and is trying to understand the God. The creator is also in the same place to being not too mathematical about itself but to attain its own conscious state. So everything is alive, everything has responsibility to itself, and everything has the conscience. The science is said to be one dream of a language which will not make sense outside of its dream.

11

INTELLECT

One needs to figure out how the world looks like today. If it asks for the religious truth then be honest. If it is playing the materialistic game then be political. If there are things that one does not understand call it God. If we get too arrogant call it an illusion. Safeguard the time and life you have with the cleverness and the wit depending on what one feels the love for. I feel love when it is natural. I do not want to determine to be in life. I need the instinct to tell me what to discern. However we all do not question if everything is Gods creation. It is and it is not. At the same time.

12

DUALITY

It is a simple concept of good and evil that pre occupies the contemporary mind. If all was simple enough we will not have the concept of time and be living in the unconstrained. Possibility is that the fragmentation of the digressive convincing argument happened somewhere, outside of our sphere of existence. So flow with the flow and evolve intellectual politics. Delegating the information to an external theory is quite an center of western thought process. But the defocus causes capitalism and the contrary communist, as a reaction to the latency of the mind.

13

SUPREME

The problem is to be untouched in our creation and the natural flavor of what we are singing and dancing. It is true if we catch up on the wit of the moment we will politically follow the mainstream not to feel for what is not ours. The human saturates with intelligence and politics and the limits. And there is the other kind, which is different in its unquestionable, but, human being susceptible does not make it the follower of the supreme Sun. The supernatural is although not as vulnerable is not quite the God to absolve the prowess of the human.

14

ADVAITA

The problem in the ancient days was the humility of certain religious people that have taken the worship of the Goddess but also maintained that their karma will absolve them from the natural law of being evaluated to be committed. It is easy to say, please feel forgiven for the frivolous human we are, and the almighty will have created us from its cosmic dream. This is Advaita, to believe the eternal dream is still uncommitted to the karma and dharma we have performed.

15

DVAITA

Contrary to the placid, we have the other variety of people humble enough to have accepted their intellect to have colluded with the forces of nature. This interaction with nature causes the human to feel the ego necessary to convince the treaty of coexistence and equally potent. This is indeed the closest approximation to what is this world. But the proportion of people that can afford to consider God and Nature as friend and not the governance is less.

16

KALIYUGA

According to the Shastra, human civilization has existed for quite some time of the four yugas, before the annihilation zeros every existence. The point is that human existence is additive in its nature. One can resolve, absolve, transcend or otherwise attrition the consciousness. If one does not commit the ritual necessary, the atma becomes eternal, subject to reincarnations and iterations. So the last part of this additive complexity is kaliyuga.

17

KALKI

Vedic scriptures had various concepts of what time is. Basic concept is that the time is situated outside of the human nature and runs a parallel. But it is possible to use time as the fulcrum of one's atma. That is to wield the human life by time. Time is like a dream in itself. Although there is the past, present and future concept, it is only human interpretation while time itself is oblivious of its nature. Kalki is the concept of one God that never happened. This concept is sophisticated.

18

PRALAYA

Human karma needs to be synchronous to dharma. Only the appropriate gets one the absolution and liberation. Rest of the committed is either ingrained in Time, or is not religious enough to be resolved in the nature. So the chaos is always increasing. The final resolution of the unresolved existence comes to a conclusion through a dissolution into the primordial ocean, this concept is called pralaya. And everything gets dissolved and the new born occurs.

19

PRIORITIES

Because of the nature of indulgence in time, it is possible to live and create orchestration of life as one opportunist feels what it needs to attain. So all the optimization creates a precedence of what one needs to attain first and which comes as a second priority. Often the digressed has almost reverse ordered the things so becomes materialistic first and religion comes next. Incorrect it is to manipulate.

20

LUCIFER

Life form and the nature of life as conceptualized in the Shastra reveals the true nature of dharma and the ensuing karma. But one has to commit the religion and the introspection to understand what is the law of the nature and what it dictates. Digression from the natural law creates a new paradigm that is not quite the way of the religious way of life. Digressed concepts are mostly seeking eternal life and flawless indulgence, which is called the Lucifer.

21

TRAIN

Existence in time causes the mind to create its own life and what it is destined to attain within a given time frame. All is possible except the religious absolution. All orchestration and activity is construed in the dream of time, occurring one thing after the other, sequentially. So it is possible to mirror what the chain of events happen when time is used and misused. This strand of existence can go forward and backward in time, and is called the thought train.

22

ALIVE

The Vedic definition of life is to attain liberation. Being alive is to commit the religious ritual and dharma. Rest of all the drama is only time and is not considered life. So there is a concept called as the value of the human. This is calculated on how qualitatively fine our atma or the consciousness is. The more sophisticated one is to live according to the correct discretion and theory, the more Ananda there is in its consciousness. This is called the joy of life.

23

DEAD

The scriptural definition only considers the quality of life and no other metrics to being alive. So all in all death is non existent. The possibilities are to attain knowledge and moksha and give ourselves into the Ananda of the Supreme. The otherwise or the digresses dissipates itself into the mirage, which does not conclude. This perpetual and eternally wandering element is called death. For practical purpose, a degraded conscious beyond a certain limit is not considered life and it only wanders.

24

TRANSCENDED

There are two levels of existence. One is the normal life that lives in conjunction with the natural forces and law. The life time completes itself according to its ways of karma and dharma. Once the completion happens the human attains the transcended state so existence which is called the atma. But it is also possible to transcend into various metaphysical levels while one is still involved in the life time. These are not the actual atma but are somehow transcended. These states are used to manipulate life.

25

GROUNDED

Grounded state of existence only conforms to living in conjunction with Nature and God. There is subtle interactions in between, but in general, do not provide the manipulation in time. If one wants to regulate the orchestrations, one needs to transcend, look at life from the observer stand point, and place itself opportunistically. What is attained through hacking the life time system is of mostly business like nature of things, only digressed, and only material.

26

SPECIES

The supreme creator has not only recommended how one needs to follow the faith. it has also created various other life forms, and the subtle interaction. The interactions among various kinds of species signifies the verity of the argument that one needs to have to determine correct path. So are the other species also contending attainment and absolution just like a human or they are creation of God? Difficult to figure out species other than human and their nature. We only have studied and manipulated the human.

27

PERSONAGE

The usual way of identity and the mirror one uses to understand and differentiate what one human is and the other, is derived by ahamkara. Although the human activity can also be ingrained in time, there is a sense of following the faith while we traverse the path. This adherence to ones own swadharma is called the personage. We all identify with what we are and what we have done using theist personage and we chase it from one life to the other instinctively. So what we identify as myself is truly transcended and guides our soul.

28

TATTVABODHA

The basic nature of human form has been subjective to study and understanding. It is not possible to create ones self out of any one particular theory. But there are definitions of almost godly nature and probable way of how God has created us. The way to understand tattva of a human is to envision how one atma creates the body and the time of doing karma. This method is used by the eternal soul to give itself a life time on this planet and what it does in its life.

29

DRIK AND DRISHYA

What a human does on this planet is not the physical karma and living through the materialistic nature of things. The philosophy only perceives. Perception so the human living in time is seen and interpreted. The limit of perception of what we understand using our entire gray matter so called the drik drishya viveka. It imposes saying there is the perceptible reality and the reality to be perceived through the vision that the transcended state of our atma has.

30

BRAHMA SUTRA

There is the composition of mind, body, senses and the soul. How all these come together is a theory called Brahma Sutra. This is not the complete reality but is an experimental way of trying to understand how God created us. Although the scriptures say it is valid to experiment only to understand God and its creation, there is the digressed that uses some ways of being born deterministically. Deterministic life forms and humans exist, but it is not complete. It is just competitive.

31

CONTEMPORARY

Because of various found and unfound theories on human life and the manipulation in time, there is considerable variety of people and there is the time fragmentation. Time has coherence and also the incoherence. Because of the unknown nature of the digressed and what it seeks, the usual hacking of life on this planet arranges things put all together in one place. From its outward appearance all things around us look to be in the same point in space and time, but naturally they occur at different time frames put together.

32

OMEN

Because of human bio diversity, there is considerable amount that one does not understand, even if one is a genius. So it is only clever to delegate what is not ones character to understand, to the forces of nature. So what guides through this maze of the good and the evil is referenced with what nature understands more than us. So looking to find an indication from the nature is the method of seeking the omen to verify what needs to be like a guidance. One needs to understand only as much as our own soul permits and rest is to be navigated using the Omen.

33

STORY

What is the highest order of putting things together is unfortunately not the time and its manipulation. The finest ways of following the nature and its omen comes about the story of our hero. Things of various natures and species and existences do interact with one another. So in all to have an abstract level of understanding mutually is to connect ones self in the middle of everything using the heroic story of our self. It is not the deterministic way of living in time that is of value. It is the story of our life that is reflected in nature.

34

PAPA

It is my belief we are still learning the ways of the goodness and trying to understand the Supreme. In the process of life we commit various karma depending on the story we are living through. All karma needs to be either dharma that we perceive at a given situation, or it needs to be absolved by nature to the level of self abnegation. We do get manipulated by time and in time. But that needs to be worn off as papa gets cleansed using the religious penance. So we need to do the ritual to do antahkarana suddhi.

35

PUNYA

The action that brings value to the only quantization that exists in this Universe, what is called the value of our conscience. It is the Punya that makes us feel the Ananda that is encoded as the destiny of our soul. There is nothing more harmony than doing the commitment as per the best estimated using out intellect and mind. We need to feel this harmony which is called the Punya, or the dharma guiding us our life and activity. This is the story so understanding the nature of the pervasive as being correct to its completion.

36

BANDHAN

We are only as sanctimonious as our story permits. Life gives us an opportunity to attain the wisdom, do the karma and feel the Ananda. But there is a lot that is happening around. Lot is interconnections exist between people and how they influence each other. There is quantization of every transaction we do with one another. This puts a fair value what we do to each other. It can not be cheated as to how much we owe to each other that creates future life in accordance to the calculation. Manipulation exists but it is only temporary in nature. The Bandhan binds us to our interactive karma unless the scores are settled.

37

PURNAM

God created various things. Each entity in this Universe has its own consciousness and its own meaning. Everything is not the same. So understanding things must happen to respecting the way the creation is according to its own character and soul. This way of thought is called completeness. The fallacy is to consider everything to be human like, but is not the actuality. So learn to accept the diversity, interact with sense of respect with all what is around. And imagine the completeness with which the Ananda prevails is all consciousness of all the things of God. Envision the completeness of our story qualitatively. This is the only conclusion that a human and the perceived.

38

NATURE

Object is human, consists of being in time and performing in what is architectural cognizance of the space inhabited. It is very exclusive to describe things in appreciation of excluding one's tangibility and describe what needs to be the attribute of anything metaphysical. It involves quite a bit more than gathering things together especially those moments that have not contributed to personal intellectual consumption. One idea is to exist in evolving a sentiment where we utter anything that is not ours. Therefore, it might be committed to a ritual to write in belief and must have been optimistic of eluding disaster as caused by nature.

39

PROGRESSION OF TIME

Ascribing destruction is primary to start anything that goes beyond what might have been termed as going well. Defining human is not considered a practice for as long as it might not have been a trend. All that is done ritually is thus similar in arrogance to value what is not dramatic. Gathering thus and inspiring the senses involved people have learned to celebrate. It is quite objective to commit one's self as not digresses and using creativity from the dispersion in universe allowing the precedence and creating it in method.

40

UNDERSTANDING

Obvious reason often described things from a basis. It might not have been possible to unite two in willful effort. They may not have described anything visible. And as with everything putting in perspective the history, people might have digressed leaving things, and forgetting. Coexistence might not have been an objective as the disintegration in social is justified as things constructing machines to perfect life as a collective theory. Time in people is described to consume and it is difficult to fathom what cannot be achieved.

41

MANAS

Still the propensity could have been quite aggressive and being logical in preclusion calculating what can be achieved. There is not much than literature in speculative that is purpose in competition of what needs to be ending philosophy. I think if people are dispersed not in integration they will get confused to build a psychological machine causing legacy. They must have seen what can be residual and what can be caught as sectarian of proliferating a particular conservative school of thought. Ritual is centric to believe the necessary instinct is to simplify happiness.

42

CONTENTION

Excluding the initiative and being smart it might be understood how to logic discretion. Social strategy is described in some other meeting like discussing life exhaustively. Despite all the unnatural content is always considering being in the middle of time, using two things. It is easy to identify beauty, and define it as wielding it into being efficient, consuming all but what is not clear is how would the destruction and dispersion will happen after the metric does not qualify as being effective.

43

STAGE

To span a civilization is important to identify what might have been objectively achieved and effort our way to believing how to answer if we felt it might be instinctive. Does not reflect modern world or may not be necessary to question some other strategy. Strategic dispersion is quite difficult at this moment if equal proportions might have been construed in quadrants if life. It is also not clear why everybody is not doing the same thing if possible. If time is a research topic one must construe purpose of this flow in our contemporary.

44

SPECULATION

If the metaphysical purpose is achieved does it contribute to determinism is something that can be doubted in the manner of respecting, quite a debate we cannot finish these days. Some people figured out that involved nature of ritual is enough to attempt describing somethings that don't cause human activity. While we are performing oblation with understanding how we prepare for respect and quality it is quite possible all the activity must have been centered with the causal that precluded human and creation.

45

UNSCIENTIFIC

The way of appreciating the origin of the force that needs decent attention and description in quite like four different things happening to cause the required burgeon. Qualitatively Devi is described as something that is in conjunction with all Vedic Gods pertinent to our civilization. Construing all the responsible forces governing nature and life and keeping human avocation in perspective we will be able to create the required to describe Devi in the manifestation unsaid. A ritual worshipping forces and in oblation to fire describing the self as performing and performing in a cultural civilization.

46

DEVI

It is important to worship energy and purity. It is important to express in cognizance. It is good to have the mannerism of life exemplified in conjunction to ethics. Devi is the Omni presence that has its own creation. We need to enumerate and quantify all we can fathom being related as an equation to let go of the understanding that will not stand alone in our perception. The creation has had a parallel and the source articulated only one side of what was created in purity. Unaware what the other half of all the creation around us. Reducing complexity of being purposeful in this place the conjunctions of elements take place.

47

ELEMENTS

Describing the necessity of water and fire, the earth and the space we characterize the Gods and Prajapati, the father. We know what is the embodiment of senses and what is the need to govern the nature and the Devas responsible for the dynamic. There is silence associated with the other side of creation from the golden womb. It is usually a dream that dissociates the practical entirety, so it cannot be practically solved. The best possible combinations elusive of more complex theories. There is only one solution in senses so there is a correlation of the example using senses and the Unknown.

48

CHANT

Ritual is not associated probably to isolate activity not knowing precedence in questioning. It depends why it is not possible to define the supreme Power, the bifurcation in Genesis, the Dream, what becomes a part of us but is also defined as the singularity in senses. Quite some activity is involved having construed a strategy. Logical evolution must have created similar identification differentiated in how the subject is compared. Reference of character is material and what needs to be created in being. Although human is represented it is typical to consider it in phonetics.

49

KAMA

Manu is also a reference communicated with if we study the necessity to offer a sacrifice. Difficult it is to preclude characters that represent isolated instance as the splendid rock is affected in its existence. The existence of proliferation is characterized if the Devas are in functional exclusion. Human life and proliferation must have been immediate after considering a few metaphysical that coexist in description. It is a practice to utter negativism as necessitated destruction needs to be caused by human. It is also important to social instinct not to be told what needs done.

50

MEDHA

Often the beginning is described as equally defining all in reference and augmenting the argument in ritual. Importance is sacrifice and the creation that happened before to enable energy to identify forces that might be not so possibly excluded everywhere else. Intellect must be having one facet. We need this uncharacterization while performing. Associated senses must have been intelligent because we never asked for it. Medha is associated to take time in describing what might cause beauty other than following. Splendid is imagining determined to take place in what we appreciate, and characters are only respected and compared with source.

51

OBLATION

Ritual is performed to justify why we need to describe. So, what happens if we do not ascribe potency or beauty to the performed. It needs to be uttered by the people that already have it so not being conspicuous of the intent or what differentiated us and what is the impetuous in our commitment. It is well understood that redundant function as intellect might not have been necessary or it is expressed in the way of an assumption like everything is the same and has characteristic optimism in considering what else can be embodied. We need to know if somethings are pure in their nature. Actually, it is also possible we might converge to believing otherwise as the exuberant is described deliberately.

52

NEURONS

Medha is responsible not to divulge as being made out of. As with the otherwise people must belong to it or else we might be mistaken. Does it ever stop being observed or we don't consider ourselves understanding how to represent ways to describe argument if we ever found out. Very protective is the nature of the response. Narayana is the manifest. It is definitely not important or possible to describe it in expression but quite an appreciation it has to be otherwise of phonetics. It probably was not intended to be beautiful like Narayana in five disparate qualities.

53

WORDS

Use of terms like Paraha is in conjunction with the name. Supposedly if we were not describing his quality we need to occupy space so that nothing else is occurring than the subject matter. Interpretation of enumerated is a possibility but again if the Vedic is itself a speculation all that needed to be done was to leave expressed as consuming more than a paradigm. Study in literature needs to be performed psychologically as we are conscious and aware as a human and if something eluded its way we definitely have one or two incorrect conjectures to help us being in place.

54

WITHIN

Position needs to be ascertained beyond doubt. Typically, scientific propensity of mistaken in determinism opens an argument of what is involved in unintended intellectual pursuit. All said it is quite elusive why manifestation in its proof exists in a dream where several are quantized leaving us with the optional way to find the objectivity. It is typically not possible to understand anything in the dream, saying human consumption must also have been interpreted as having no history.

55

LOGIC

As yet we still need to find where they want us to lose or use discretion. Dispersion is bound to have an explanation and darkness comes about to be the medium. Therefore, if we are truly committed to belief we must be able to be equivocal. If dispersion occupies space typically also it is in the process of logic to defeat. Otherwise we will not have questioned the intent that worked. I think there are a few negativisms as a part of what cannot be criticized as the criticism must have been a part of the question and possibly containing some amount of truth usually consumed in oblations.

56

THINK

Existence must have included us in the ocean, so we call the effort to use out physical existence. Other than focus on human body the Nasadiya hymn does not reveal anything that cannot be achieved including an answer to a question and the creation. The form of elemental is not defined as it is either a subject of thought or the structure. If studied Nasadiya can possibly answer what is the basic incompleteness in the human. Logic is downplayed and always the respectful conjecture is qualitative matter that is quite tangible wherever it has been. Also, it is not clear if some processes go either way and may be incoherent to our existence.

57

SRI

Thus, if we use respectful ritual it is sufficing to keep things alive. Opulence is related to the vision in discerning the good light from the bad. Identifying thus we need to respect the possible sources rich. It is quite possible human discretion is contained in Sri. Lakshmi is associated with activity. The worship of Sri is fulfilled by the descendants of the primary race as she exudes white light. This centering our attention to activity, brightness, discretion, the war against asuras, and the desire to fulfil the Vedic Duties, we will be able to worship in the ritual. It is also described what is sufficient is vision or being a visionary and quite an inactivity in silence is also a good quality.

58

LAKSHMI

Wealth is not transaction and qualitatively we can only perform, and Sri is not characterized in adjectives other than being imagined with Vishnu. Human being exists because of the things construed in the past. The probable way to describe existence is to present alternatives. Vedic probably described Purusha with some amount of impetus. Human life could not have been a target to achieve as the intellect was solving something else. Human is also not associated or bound to actions such as ritual and the disconnects survives to define religion. We are surrounded by people that have achieved and defined things of abstract beauty and the necessary objects required in an otherwise are all available at disposition.

59

PURUSHA

Purusha is descendent of Narayana. If the position is unoccupied we might think all has eluded to define everybody at the same time. In time only, people will realize who they are. There seems like five odd types of humans ranged between negation and descendent. To define Purusha you need to use Purushena or Paurusha. There is some characterization here that can imprint the time and place of such a belief or composition, a bit more accurate that calling them as being critical when necessary. Another type of characterization is conversational, difficult to understand if we are contained in a conversation.

60

RITUAL

Absolving is easy if we find the way to understand the following. If necessary, we will be quiet in the ritual not understanding the Sruti itself in the place of oblation. Sthita is the Manas and the responsible witnessed the law. Respect thus obtained in time will be pronounced in respect for the desire determined to come aware of our character. Describing this where these are located we will then think of the plausibility of description that occurred without the conscious and also several other ways of worship. The possible ways are just describing what is not discussed when the alternative is presented as the well construed by one's talent to present an alternative argument surviving time.

61

INVOLVEMENT

Time is in serious correlation even with what can be explained other than what is happening. In the event of being present because of the forces only we need to think the complexity that might be not inclusive to begin with. All that is offered is to consume the abode of Genesis. We will give the righteous to the wellbeing and this will create the possible way we have talked to each other and in the scenario presented there is nothing but solved. Solution thus is to take time being the subject to what we are and what is consuming.

62

DURGA

Beyond cognitive is personage in deifying the place we construe. Certain manifest occurs as a reaction to what we do. Durga is the end of reason. Presenting alternative is questionable. Probably purity must have been a primary search for existence to depict the minimal conjecture not to reach completeness. Fire is the source of the mindful and we will offer the dwelling so associated verbal is not directed to things that exist in a karma. Durga is associated with things committed during our life as such we need to determine to exclude what is known. Presenting alternative at source has been negated in logic since there is not much vibrant to lead us to dissolving.

63

PERSPECTIVE

Karma is pertinent and do it again to pray the conclusion. If we define the surroundings we may find ourselves in the silence. Why is it disparate and even exclusive as a unified thought of appreciating the nature and its splendor? Indirect it is after we include ritual to have been performed well every time. This is the prayer of conclusion of the place of worship is confined. Purity is the character. There is quite bit of qualitative in connecting the verse chanted in ritual. We need to think why discrete mathematics should be derived from inspiration.

64

SPOKEN

All said how many numbers are associated covering the subject digressed as untold. There is a deep thought that is ascribed to the Nakshatra. If enumerating is style of the source to be determined as a psychology, we need to understand it using five adjectives that coincide the probable reason why they committed to connect during a ritual. Why is there a possibility while we are bound by duty to prescribe what is defining the obliterated? Thus, defying quantity in a question, we can certainly define position in committed and probable digression from religion.

65

DISASTER

Nakshatra is defining characterization probably left out to witness us as carrying legacy but we need to be precise in considering if all around us is what is consumed in space. Typical concern is not to engrave anything in subject trying to not being the doer of telling how the oblation has come into effect after what we say. We are not centered. Neither we occupy space and time. Performing ritual has come about as a thing we progress into probably how equal proportion is interpreted. Vishnu thought something, and the causal is attributed to some image that we persist.

66

DREAM

In the nature we must be dispersing what we observe being the latent but yet being descriptive of the character it must find its form. Describing Vishnu, the formless characterization that we dwell to come into existence as everything has its character. Due to the violation Vishnu is imagined to be sublime to persist on a meaning to form what is dual in beauty. This critique will create a cyclical but aware of the oblation we will descent our image. In spite purity being in place we will need to feel the light being the source and the rest being a way of the descended to say when it happens we will have the progressive unless we put a thought to it.

67

NARAYANA

There is quite a bit common in considering beauty. Thus, the Juhomi is supposedly assuming beauty is people around are consuming anything. We need to describe at this instance if the definitions are similar a similar or arcane to characterize what will attain Narayana. According to Vedic stating Vishnu in the performer being identified we do not seek anything Rudra is attributed in the skill to perform. Performance is governed with an intent to characterize beauty as Narayana or subjective as in Rudra. Similar thought process must dwell around us to not question composition in a condition what precludes people elsewhere not be a part of the intent ful.

68

RUDRA

Rudra is mostly to sublime if we have an opinion during the oblation, therefore Vedic starts with definition of the objective being appreciating the equation that consumed anything other than all the prehistoric that might surface as future or the performer is allusive in all character to be equal to the inclusive. Rudra this inclusive of appearance will think if all was not identified then we will need to attain the possibility of all inclusive to perseverance of the thing we are about to commit. It is conclusion that is probably not proportioned as the impetuous will be responsible to define it as a thing in personage we might be the oblivion.

69

SUPREME

The imagination is inhabited and needs to image itself so long as Rudra is supposed in diversity apart from differentiated identifying talking and thinking animosity that we are intended to carry forward. It is the character of Rudra to come about after all our imaginations have either unheard or our imagination in in parallel to what we can understand with our oblation. Human instinct is imaginative and also it is accepted that inclusive of the philosophy, we can define nonexistence. Conclusion in human life is imagined to be non existent. To discuss the illuminated source is the beginning to the question. If intellect is embodied, it will have its effect but needs to be delivered in oblation. The purpose discussed in education should lead to life in speculation as the matter is pervasive in space.

70

VISHNU

This characterization typically what considers the anti thesis to containing knowledge or defining or listening. The end of life is to subject the imaginative to the complete extant. The prayer of completeness is experienced, and we will need to perform the ritual and say it to be heard by the Sun. Being is defined by the place. Situated thus Narayana is governing the nature to nurture. The precedence to human being is disconnected from life during the ritual. Why should the pervasive assume character of the precedence constituting life or the being. It is thus assumed that the persistent is the nature we derive. Brahma associated with Narayana is different in the forceful nature of position. Life is characterless as it does not occupy space.

71

TRINITY

Thus, the manifesting is situated to characterize the matter. We need to attain the character of the forces that are governed by Rudra, Brahma and Narayana. The only position left is the place of worship and oblation associated with their character. It is easy to say all the non existent may not be derived for the place we can identify as the abode. The precedence is linear in nature as deriving the effort in four forms. Defining lineage, placing the devas and Purusha in ritual, chanting shlokas invoking energy, and relations of man and woman in the light. From deriving the beginning, to Prajapati, the presented is assumed to not have caused the human as well. Forces are derived from each other.

72

DELUSION

The ocean that created the matter, the forces arranging themselves, the character of creating Genesis. Thus, the assumption is it is a matter of opinion to either consider a theory inclusive in spite of the question. A definition should suffice the existential habit we have. Thus, defining the position of devas, we associate the Purusha as the being not representing individual but the activity of worshipping the fire. We need to identify and include the responsible devas and the Purusha in conjunction invoking the relentless forces that are derived from our conscious. It is understood all the existent is invoking and representing these forces with the senses involved in oblation.

73

SKY AND EARTH

There is no conjunction between a man and a woman without the intellect. Intellect defines the union and progeny dedicated to performing ritual. May the intellect be present during our lifetime. To happen is to commit. We think there are various ways to describe relationship given being consumed in time. The concept of time manifests itself during the creation of the metaphysical world in conjunction. There really is no speculation considering we can witness the place without causality. The sky is uttering to the earth. The fire is created including the nature of water. Human soul is connected to the space we breathe.

74

COMMUNICATION

The intellect is associated with the respect to the Sanskrit spoken clearly. It is also said the purity associated with all the activity in unison cannot create the space as persistent but what happens after it us understood with the connection. This conjunction of the human being with the matter around us causes the fulfilment. The question is can we witness anything not uttered in oblation. I pay my respects to my antecedents and the aspiration associated with duty. The purpose in manifest is expressed as contemplation of the equation to have existed given all against us or not constituting us.

75

BLISS

The Ananda is defined as the thing that is outside observing the highest form of interaction. To interact is the condition satisfied, during oblation. Must have been persistent to perform at will. Not clear if the difference in people is stark given the source. It is thus possible the construe a perfect race in this civilization. The destruction itself must have caused the other and we need to understand it as the beginning philosophy. It is not clear how persistent life copies the perfect. Therefore, fragmenting characteristics to the approximate will cause a disconnect necessary to copy which is the source of the solution. Given this nature of completeness, the correct form of existence must have manifested itself in either being respectful of the happiness, intellect, the commitment, the resource and the human being the performer of the ritual. It is not possible not to do anything. This the force the brings people close in discretion of opportunity.

76

RESPECT

Pure systems are characterized in complexity and dependence. This is quite the nature of what is left undone. The complexity is that the offering is to the nature being interactive. Human intelligence can be paralleled but not as a description thus being the one who knows the nature of creation. Nature in its composition needs to be communicated with and this it is mindful we need to describe the faith inclusive of all considered important for being required and adequate in qualitative and quantitative to prove it is the best possible permutation.

77

FREEDOM

It is quite interpretative to study a ritual that represents their composition. What that inspires us is we can be impersonating the different nature that may have evolved. It is quite possible to fragment the entirety and prove all it takes for the parallel as it will not be convincing to try being them. It is good in the way of finding what else they may not describe to let us know it is a thing of the past. All that they are made up is the oblation, the interaction, the personage, intellect to have a relationship and achieving perfection. Speculative philosophy is an inclusive considering it is an opinion formed in comfort. If they prove parallelism we need to prove another paradigm similar to the scale of precedence, the cause for explanation.

78

EVOLUTION

Vedic religion was situated, and they expressed. The discussion is centered to certainty of the imagined. Allusion to Gods, is a cohesion of effort. All happened is delivered in recognition of lineage, nomenclature and the momentum of the existence quite not driven by the performer. It is evident they correlate intellect to advantage in understanding how to address why things happen not subject to change for example. Human activity is also paralleled with the willingness to oblation. Life is substantiated with food. But quite not the literal to understand the works. I believe the subject of relentless and intellect, even wellbeing, imaginative technology evident is all subject to dissociate.

79

SUBLIME

They probably did not verbalize functional importance as much as what it should be called. All that happens must happen by the impetus notwithstanding the way things descend into being. Associated thus the Purusha must be described materially willing to perform the transaction. It is not clear if the creation or the creative description ever stopped causing us to just being intellectually present and perform all that has already happened. It is a belief that creation is subject to what can be imparted as education or even a ritual. Thus, no activity is any different that reciting. Must be true that it is a sufficient condition to coexist. The matter is constituted of truth. The transcended is sublime till we are able to comprehend the entire orchestration to Brahma.

II

STATE OF THE ART

80

METAPHYSICAL

Let us start from somewhere in the middle. Somewhere where everything in this world is going on easily. Let us just agree for the time being that the Truth is in the Metaphysical. Is it because of tangibility or is it because the mistake is easy or is it because it is difficult to celebrate simplicity. To tell you what the metaphysical is easy and to criticize the existent Philosophy is difficult. Having given the disclaimer let us start with the undiscussed territory.

Let us start to think on any subject matter and hit a wall truly and diligently. It is necessary for the metaphysical. Metaphysical is the underlying simplicity upon which we do mistakes or get it correctly. Because the metaphysical says it does not matter either way. It is easy to exemplify it in language or meaning because we anyway do not understand anything to begin with. Does nature have its own way to protect itself despite our frivolity or our otherwise. Is the common ground of Metaphysical unfair for our vehemence or is it way too intelligent?

Metaphysical is not divinity as much as it as a common conjecture to live within a restrictive philosophy and still being able to create life or thought or experience or a direct parallel to the ideal. Still I believe that what we have is enough to attain the supreme being and that in an idyllic situation we may want not to believe in ourselves and delude our intelligence and simplicity to the emotional contribution of the metaphysical than saying that I see that the ending is like this or beginning is like this or everything should be like this.

81

ABSTRACT

Why is it important to abstract? Is it because we have made it too difficult to ourselves or is it because it is the correct way to represent let us just say a particle in a chaos. Abstract is fundamental that says I do not have to subjectivise everything. Abstract is also correctness just because it is better than analysis.

I want to understand what is important. To miss something or not having heard about it or to know that abstract is always functional to minimize our indulgence and create an alternative for volition. Abstract is a way to function where the importance of substandard existential can be ignored in order to value mind more than the actuality. Because the actuality whether you like it or not may have been a product of unfinished business to begin with.

Abstract is not impersonalization. In a way it is a little bit more purist than the existentialism around. Because it says that we can flatten the thought process, or we can flatten the unnecessary, glorify ourselves and get into the abstract and feel better because I know who created the unnecessary. Because the unnecessary exists as a paradigm than a solvable… abstraction is the only way to understand that neither you created it nor I.

82
LIFE

Life my dear friends is a particle. An ideal principle that is buried in the ingredients of the perceivable or the unperceivable of the quantities of temporal and experiential administration of time. We all get administered with the 24-hour thingy. Where life gets administered is difficult to say. Are we life… are we complete… or are we alive qualitatively to compete with the simplified nature of this life particle.

Elusive the life particle is. Duality is a proof of life in the way of saying that the blandness of the time artifact we live in is subjective and the embedded life particle is not. We have the option to exercise but the puristic administration may or may not reveal even qualitatively where the life particle is and where the conditional subjectivity of the human tangible is in time we all have.

We essentially are incomplete, and life takes care of it in its own way. May be the point is to become fully alive at the end but how is anybody's guess. We can revel, we can do, we can get everything, but everything is something with life being an embedded principle elusive of even the rightest of the freedom we may have to make it better.

83

SIMPLICITY

There are a few problems in life that can be satisfied under one condition. When you once solve one of those problems you understand the nature of the unconstrained. The thought or the process cannot be subject to temporal spectrum of the range of experiential. What brings our mind to not revel in this range of Life. When do we understand the simplicity?

Can we simplify the entire if that was the initial condition or even for that matter destiny? Why do we do somethings with volition and why do we perceive quality instead of quantity in a given fragment of life. Everything one way or the other can be simplified to glorify either meditation or silence or beauty or just matter of factly the selfishness embedded in the human mind to react to the directness of simplicity. Glorify this or that the simplicity must show up as a tangible.

84

PARTICLES

Individuality most often cannot be represented in our civilization. It must have been better that our over constrained human effort to embody the redundancy. Still individuality as a paradigm of the tangible in terms of the purpose of life cannot be great also. In considering civilization with any thought needs certain amount of the abstract. Let us call this intellectual tangibility of clarity of a near to idyllic representation as not an individual but a civilizational particle.

It is easier to talk about the abstract and a particle in one sentence. It also takes care of the complexity of the unpublished representations of wonder as to how orchestrations happen. Anyway, to be civilizational particle is not an achievement as much as it is a philosophers or a meditators effort to not overcrowd one's mind into wondering about everything and anything that happens around. Particles have character and a duty to perform. You understand self and responsibility to one's self once you get to be a civilizational particle.

85

CIVILIZATION

Let us just say at this point that our civilization is everything. There is no point having another parallel civilization like this isn't it. There must be other civilizations. A philosopher who can solve an abstract can definitely come to one conclusion. That is that perfectness that is a philosophical condition for us may be actuality for other parallel civilizations.

Is civilizational interchange possible? If not, then what is our mistake. No there is no mistake. It is just like this. Once you grow up to be a good particle you can visit other civilizations also. Up until then we must do our due diligence and not buy Hollywood ideas of experiential and grandeur. Otherwise it will be a waste of time. Not to be so critical at this point we are all OK and the civilization is also OK in a Ritam stand point. It is just that there may be something extra in our civilization like time and there is incompleteness in our Mind space to sustain the entirety.

86

VEDA

In general, the Veda must have come from the Vedic Civilization as a parallel and not as history. If treated like this then we know what is Veda. Huge tomes of text may not have been the Veda after all. It is easy to lose oneself at the slightest inclination towards thinking that although verity of the Veda and Vedic Civilization can be proved qualitatively one cannot afford to say that what we have at hand is fake.

Vedic Civilization was very simple, almost tangible in some of their speculative ideologies as ours. They may have had another way to represent time. They may have created another layer of activity within the framework of the Metaphysical. They may have had no redundancy leaving us to take care of our own Vedic study. Time spent in ritual and appreciation may have been more direct in oneness with their nature than an avocation.

They might not talk to us in person but certain ideas of Ritam may be construed I don't know how. We may not have digressed but that is the way we are. It does not stop us from redoing the Veda in a simpler manner. If given a chance I would have wanted to meditate myself in the Vedic Civilization.

87

SPECULATIVE PHILOSOPHY

Unconditional thought can be afforded in our Civilization. In general, this is called Speculative Philosophy. Everything else is preconditioned and orchestrated… nicely… carefully… precisely… and wonderfully. We do not have an option to avoid either from an intellectual stand point but the beauty of it is that we are free as anything else in the Ritam. Freedom is not Speculative Philosophy. I do not clearly know how it works but there is an equilibrium to the ideas contained within and the unconditionality coming from both the directions in terms of one Civilizational achievement. Speculative Philosophy is more transactional and encompasses subjects like technology, administration, system and most importantly Civilizational promise if there is any.

If given an option I would do Speculative Philosophy for its openness in any given constraint and get my meditation from the Vedic Civilization so as to get an equilibrium. This is a vast topic and can be subject to discussion more effectively than what we have done with the Veda is my guess on it… you people can take your own guesses. It is easier to overcome language and reach philosophical silence in Speculative Philosophy is my experience in time.

88

EXEMPLIFICATION

Our Civilization is communicative. We are subject to experientialism because that is the way we think of presentations, interactions, personalities, our past and our present. We often become subjective to the mirror. Therefore, correct subjectivity as an impersonal introspection leads to a way of understanding better termed as exemplification. Ideally, we want to liberate ourselves from misrepresentation. Often direct self interpretation of any particle or an example of situation or even the nature of surroundings can be abstracted to a nonfunctional endeavor and exemplification comes around as more appropriate term to our own disinterest to want to think or not to think of let us just say a mirror oriented interpretation of life in general. Therefore, exemplification is a substandard philosophical condition.

89

SUBJECTIVITY

Ritam is what we should idealize. Therefore, everything in our life becomes subjective in this particular way of philosophy. Subjectivity is a thing and not a person. Therefore, any effort to understand anything leads to the abstract nature that lends all the artifacts as a subjective putting abstract and subjectivising what needs to be made easier than it could have been by drawing unnecessary parallels and squandering our respect. We cannot put our effort just as yet deifying anything in our lives. A particle realizing let's say meditation for example must have been focusing beyond and therefore subjetivising everything in between. It would have been great if people give in to each other not as walking and talking psychologies but the freedom that is needed to put the subtlety of respect that we want to give for subjectivity. It is easier to respect a subject.

90

SCIENCE AND TECHNOLOGY

Science and technology are Metaphysical artifacts that have found their place in our lives. There are a few levels to it. What happens in the middle is a trickling down effect from the point of qualification to direct application in our life. There is also the tangible and the non-tangible aspects to it. Either way the effort put into the science and technology by various educational institutions as well as various companies is not representative of how a technological idea gets incubated and then the already created trickles down mostly untouched.

Just as any other idea science and technology is just the way it is. I do not know why we do it, but it is there. Our Civilization does not question much as much as one would realize that most of tangible or non-tangible ideas may be more satisfying if we are able to appreciate the abstract ease of a good engineering example and leave it at that. We have our own way of creating is what I am saying. Most of it is unuseful for meditation or learning.

91

LOGIC

Logic is of three types. Before we present what logic is we need to simplify our perspective of understanding life. Having dumped the redundancy and having arranged for a good initiative into understanding how life is or could have been logic is a way of almost saying how it is.

Negation is a first kind of logic where the human mind is put up against an artifact. What we then say the if it is not that simple then either it is not let's just say a creation of human mind. Next comes the more abstract geometric logic that brings in into perspective the cyclicality or linearity or flatness of various puzzles and put more reason into the already happened. Third form of logic is a layered structure of saying that what cannot be singularized in one shot must have been because of a primary layer of the abstract purity and a secondary layer of human configuration as senses or the experiential.

92

MACHINE

Once upon a time we used to live in the boundless space. Then our Civilization happened. What is all that goes on. Is it idealistic or is it the ideal and a structure? This ubiquitous structure is what the machine is. The machine brings tangibility and puts a high from of a pattern to everything that can be done in the Civilization

Is machine self existent even without any particles living in it. Does machine bring in parallelism that addresses all the redundancy however simple our lives are. Machine brings mathematics and geometry and replace the temporal experiential of a particle in the Civilization. We are fully embodied representations that can carry something out into a more ideal scenario and in a way value the same thing in let's just say as complete.

93

EXPERIENTIALISM

Experientialism is most often a failed Philosophy or somebody's interpretation of life and someone that might have thought that it must have been like that. Even if the experience is good or even divine there may be a barrier and if we become better we could leave the experiential behind and live in the ideal.

Experientialism might have microcosmic effect, or it might mean that there is an entire bunch of people that buy the same Philosophy and adhere to it after they have experienced it. But I would leave everything behind if I perceive that someone has gotten somewhere in the effort to understand life just because I do not have time to compete or criticize unless it is perfect or more beautiful and apt to embrace it or let myself to believe that someone somewhere must be definitely having it better... so much as to taking life into an unfathomable simplicity that agreeing with people or the experiential.

94

MANAGEMENT STRUCTURES

We often do not care how much time we waste. Civilizational particles have unanimously agreed to live and present themselves in a way almost two times. The first agreement could have been freedom exercised to sign up for the civilization. The second is subjectivising ourselves to various artifacts of limits and experiential. This is called a management structure. There is absolutely no way of criticizing it more that getting around it.

Management structures are also metaphysical like science and technology at their point of implementation. They effect people and psychologies almost to an extent of bringing in orchestration as a matter of the exercisable or adherence. It gives us something like an option to choose either way and make us subjective to anyone that is looking into say freedom or a question or something like a complete ununderstandable and say that it was their choice to be doing what they are doing the relevential being only the decision making algorithm.

95

PRECEDENCE

Precedence is a good way of getting out of incorrect philosophy or even logic. Logic or Philosophy needs a typical surface to be placed upon. What we are saying is that if something has existed before me or even something the incorrectness may not be attributed to the latter.

Does it mean that the mistake might have happened in the first place? May be may be not all I am saying is that Civilization could have been OK and that if I ever want to unlearn everything the civilization had to offer I would be OK form the Ritam stand point and that I will not take myself into a void space and be completely wiped out. There is no void space at all and everything must stop at a good baseline.

96

EXTRATERRESTRIAL AND BEYOND

We have already talked about parallel Civilizations. I bring in this point not to exemplify the greatness of other Civilizations as much as wanting to distinguish between what is the normal civilizational way of thinking and how to identify a thought let us say that could be attributed to the Extraterrestrial.

Human mind and Civilizational thoughts are most often emotional whether you want it or not. We also have disassociated thoughts going around. The extraterrestrial thoughts are most often a bit more embodied with a sense of let's just say completeness. In the way of saying how the Rig Veda starts with the Yagi doing Yagna being one with the fire that is probably a simple form of respect.

97

DUALITY

Duality is a way of saying that somehow or the other we can get away from being judgmental about the correctness and the wrongness. There exists a fair abstract ground to base the civilization and the dichotomic experience. The limitation of the idea of duality is that you are saying it does not matter not once but twice. Might as well focus on Swadharma or Meditate despite logicists reveling on how we have made up a story of right and wrong and still exist eternally.

98

BEGINNING AND ENDING

What happens when a philosopher starts to think of the beginning or the ending is like signing up to a temporal thought constructs instead of great actualities. Anything that has a beginning or ending is essentially cheating at some point or the other. Let us just say that if anything else has a beginning or ending other than time is to say that beginning and ending might as well be the same.

The point most often is to mind one's own business and focus on the continuum. Continuum says that we probably can abstract ourselves from the Civilizational machine or at some point the Civilizational machine will exist without any of us being in it… as a standalone artifact in the space and time. If we have gotten into it we can get out of it… just don't know when.

99

STATE OF THE ART

State of the art is Philosophy in its most independent manner glorifying the individuality as well as the civilizational machine. To be able to interact with the matter and material as an abstract and sharing a perspective. Nature is not state of the art. Light is a state of the art and Gayatri Mantra is state of the art. To be able to ignore particles around and find meditative dynamic that is not wanting characterizing in duality is also state of the art. State of the art is being ready to clarify even if the Civilization might exemplify the morose.

100

MIND SPACE AND HUMAN MIND

Mindspace is, is self sustenance. Dependency is everywhere. When we have not grown up to such an extent it is difficult to argue with the proponents of failed Philosophy. We are not in the business of qualitatively analyzing every particle that has exercised freedom to interact to begin with. Mind space is self while the general space is participative at its own risk. What is the risk… may be to sustain a mistake is not mind space and a human mind?

Human mind when alive and interactable and not a celebrated exclusive has a little bit of potential that can be exercised in a general sphere of existence. There are a few likeables and if you don't like it then the doer is at his or her own risk. The potential of risk taken to subjectivise anything cannot be reflected. When a celebrated specie tends to think it is manifest in a disillusionment and not as a symbiotic solution sphere. We can ignore bad examples in terms of surreal accountability to what we want to pursue. We want to follow at the least bit the human mind that chases logic at its minimum.

101

TIME

Human mind perceives time only when there is a repeat... rest is all a mirror because we cannot do better... at least we don't give a bad example. Qualitatively all the time is personal time except for the analysis unwelcomed.

Time is created for us. We waste time. Therefore, there is time. We can only meditate and not educate people on becoming phenomenal. Let the society evolve to time and compete with it while we spend our time typing text for example.

Let us bring sequentiality. If there is quality time has meaning. Time gives in into influencing self and other people around. It is not a great feat. We can do our qualitative analysis and get over with revelers of this Civilizational artifact as time with ease. If anything is a disconnect with what we don't like it is time and the freedom others have exercised to wield time as heroism.

102

SWADHARMA AND NORMATIVENESS

Swadharma is the condition to having figured it out. May be Harvard has figured it out, but it is also a presentable fact ology instead of becoming participative. What Swadharma is saying is once we have figured out the random nature of administrated life we are going to pull it out of our antahkarana and adhere to it as if it was not our business to having put in the spectrum of the Civilizational experiential. Normative ness is normal beauty that gets administered as well. We may want to find out how normal is it to be original. Being original in social sphere is acquiescing to the fact that it may be wanting to communicate outward to the original listener. We want to satisfy outward condition than we want to revel in the perfectness of a Civilizational Creation. Normal is not knowing what we adhere to when we have cracked the adherential.

103

EXISTENT AND NON-EXISTENT

Let us say that thought exists, and that activity exists… how does it exist. Does it exist as metaphysical nebula that can be traversed by a human particle. If I had an option would I still be traversing thought and activity incessantly. First let us see if any of this occupies space. Does matter so tangible occupy space or it is also a sensory activity.

Unless we do a qualitative analysis as to what we like we cannot comment whether any of what we live is existent or nonexistent. Qualitative analysis also can prove what is realizable. Can we stop our analysis and quandary if we stumble on a future promise of let's say a good quality space or light that does not contain the thought and activity navigation's? Will we ever get this message let us say from the outside of the containment of the existent and the nonexistent.

104

INCORRECTNESS

We can assume we are correct up until we stumble upon an initiative. Human initiative of course of let's say analyzing or criticizing or even for that matter making it better like a future promise through may be exercising option of a volition state of consciousness. Of course, again all this is incorrect because there should never have been an introspective phase to make ourselves or surroundings better.

Is incorrect a judgment. Does it defeat or glorify purposefulness? By purpose what I mean is that can a human mind ever accept qualitatively a state of meditativeness that we may have to wait indefinitely to be wanting to make it better. There is a good amount of volition as a human effort than just saying as a guided student that something is incorrect. I think incorrect exists for its own sake. We cannot draw our inspiration from it.

105

INCOMPLETENESS

Meanwhile when I am waiting indefinitely to let us say a change in the surrounding that does not prompt me to question of criticize or spend an effort. Whatever takes effort must have been incomplete in some way... very beautifully. What is the beauty in incompleteness. Because if a human initiative or a qualitative aspect of the surrounding dynamic is complete then we will have a difficult time as theorists.

Freedom exists because of incompleteness. There is always a fair ground to leave anything fully realized or leave it unrealized. If we have a common conjecture or an agreement on qualitative incompleteness will it allow us to do our due diligence and reach the state if Swadharma. While doing our Swadharma will we ever ask ourselves that what is the absolute state or moment of or even the right place and time to get something complete. There is so much inspiration in the incomplete.

106

DISCONNECTS

While I am diligently following by ideas on incorrectness and incompleteness do I stumble upon opinions. What is a good way to look at these opinions that our surrounding may have to offer. Is there a metaphysical that controls their flow of opinions? If a metaphysical exists to redundify superfluity of opinions is there some sort of disconnect. Disconnect is like this… I may not have to exercise volition into participativeness out of any instigative behavior from the outside.

If surroundings are not representative for complete embodiments of particles doing their due diligence there may be two kinds of disconnects. The interfering thoughts might not have any embodiment… so they may exist in a fake space of parallelism. Next is to consider other particles or individuals around and simply conjecture on as to what their mutual sense of responsibility is. There must be a connect and a disconnect facility to take up qualitative negation bringing our focus on what we want to do and let the surroundings have the freedom to interfere or abstractly orchestrate what they perceive as popular. We will definitely have disconnects and have good perception of embodiment.

107

STORY

Story is more enthusiastic than connects or disconnects. Most of abstract philosophy can identify patterns of unrealism. Unrealism is subject to our propensity, disposition or even treating the surroundings more respectfully. What is unreal always gives us freedom to ignore entire socio psychological beliefs and themes, most often history and even for that matter biological functions. Story and opinion exists on everything, every subject because a precedence is needed for the sake of its own mostly. What happens when you very subtlely and uncritically choose to focus on something else than the story. Many things can happen and come from the surroundings. Surroundings may or may not realize that you are not buying the story. You may just say that first there is a disconnect and second that I will exercise volition on the qualitative aspect of participating in a story even if I had to. After all despite all this around we must have a good idea of how to minimize our effort and do the easy things for ourselves like meditate or pursue qualitative knowledge.

108

FAILURES AND CYNICISM

Simplicity or simplifying initiative will fail in the light of failures and human propensity of cynicism. I am not saying that it is good or bad to be cynical for just a while in our lives when we fail on something that we value. What will happen is two things. First, we will know that what needs to be realized will realize itself and we can stop being cynical.

Next part is tricky. Surroundings may land up exemplifying their own similar failures. Next thing they may do is a very strong background in cynicism and present an opportunity to join an initiative that may have a completely altogether different dictionary. Who knows whether to respect grand failures in the surroundings and their cynicism. As long as we did not mislead them we will have enough honesty to ourselves.

109

PURPOSE OF LIFE AND CELEBRATIVENESS

Purpose of Life is according to one Civilization contain the celebratedness of the entirety. Some organizations in our Civilization celebrate... does it mean that we have perspectivized the entirety. Or are we the same old descendants of some great past civilization. Purpose of life is not to finish anything for as long as I can be honest. Celebratedness depends for the time being on who the participants are.

Purpose of life in our versatile civilization is to identify... define... and exercise volition on our adherences and qualitatively identify ourselves to our sake as well as for the sake of particles around that may have done their due diligence. Therefore, getting back to celebratedness... it is of a great value not to characterize a function of celebration but taking it as a great opportunity to deify and liberate the participants to reflect what needs to be reflected in terms of the entirety that needs to be qualified in a more abstract form. For many particles around entirety in this Civilization is not everything. That brings quality to our celebration.

110

EXCLUSIVITIES AND SOCIAL ORGANIZATIONS

There are various artifacts in our Civilization. Social organizations are a bad example and exclusivity is a good example. Invoking a particular socio psychological emotion and popularity and criticism are essential characters of a social organizations. My point is how can we justify embodiment when the entirety of the exemplified social organizational behavior may represent a random self-gratification. Exclusivity is more often my subject of thought and a centered philosophy. I cannot avoid here to mention that there is a little more philosophy that goes into the volition to be exclusive. Most often post philosophical conditions are metaphysical. Metaphysical simplifications and exclusivities exist… functionally I don't know. As with some other subtleties that exist exclusivity is something at this point of my life that I respect as an outsider and represent in my way of communicating and adhering to thoughts and the existent surrounding in the way of showing care and discerning.

111

PSYCHOLOGY AND BOMBS

First there needs to be a philosophical conjecture on the way of how dictionary evolves… on how most of that is tangible in the text book as well as in life in general has gone through a sort or evolution in a human psychology. Human psychology and discretion have been exercised into various things good and bad… and coincidentally most of it could have been mental and in a good way to limit my cynicism. There is not much we can do against a philosopher negating stories of tangibility but most of the celebrated heroisms and adventures are pretty much surreal. Still there is a lot of effort into let's say what matters. Therefore, if a bomb destroys what does not matter then it is a good example. If a bomb destroys a matterful mental aspect of an individual or a group that is considered tangibly important in the way of saying that if you do not value this what else is there to value… is also a good thing.

112

GOD

Once upon a time the redundancy of language emerged in confronting atheism. I avoided closeness to these surrounding and focused on Philosophy.... up until I came across this statement... God does not take part in our sin or virtue. The goodness of God cannot be represented than personal intellect accepting anything else for that matter.

The critical factor in us must limit itself to duality and the qualitative opinion must always be abstracted to a mirror. Most of the particles have not evolved so much after all to even understand these principles. Let us not wait for them to catch up. God must be an embodiment and present more like an existent along with a surreal parallelism not waiting to be subjectivised by human beings in their daily conclusivities. If we can overcome and understand subjectivity, then it is possible to build upon a relationship with God. It depends on the let's say the stream of focus we can evolve for example Swadharma.

113

SPACE

Space is a special space. Embodiment of the inverse of a void space will run a parallel to the definition of space. We are particles and contribute to our minimization of thought and tangible streams of unrealizable data. Space is more of a philosophers God. Space is also the qualitative epitome of sophistication of our selves.

Space is constituted of space. Space embodies a stationaryism from where we can derive or thoughts and tangibles. A good civilization does and cannot represent adherential value anymore… there is no duality… and one thing is not better than the other. I often used to say that life in some civilizations only has two layers… first is space and next is the intellect that brings this space into the manifest. Unlike our popular linguistic jargon space and its manifest will not have time. Quality exists and the proof of existence of the Manifest comes from space and the proof of space comes from the manifest.

114

PARALLELISM

I do not have opinions on many things around… and to top it off there are so many things around. How is that possible. Have I interacted so much in time and mind to have so much clutter. In a civilization where duality exists parallelism is almost like God. Parallelism takes care of orchestration in general saying the nature of manifest in some civilizations cannot be subject to qualitative entirety. Every activity imposed by any particle must run a parallel. Our adherence is limited to Swadharma. We may not know exactly our value but isn't it good to have not an opinion and judge ourselves if we can delegate philosophically to parallelism. Surprisingly we will find that silence does not have a parallel… therefore if we come around anything inspiring we need to become that.

Parallelism is the best that any Philosophy can get in our Civilization. Parallelism will also not leave us with a void when we are done.

115

DIFFICULTY AND MEMORY

Difficulty is underderstanding of duality let's just say. I have no idea as to why anything is difficult as long as it is consequential. The surroundings usually have an etiquette of normal imposed behavior. Difficulty in an abstract term is the surroundings understanding a little bit more than that you have. Often in one's life the difficulty is the only proof of the existence of the machine instead of a surviving Civilization. Because it is easy for you and me to understand.

Difficulty is more personified than human value. Sustaining a negated fact or an emotion can often be clad in difficulty. So, when you face anything difficult… act smart. There is no conclusivity in difficulty. There is no difficulty there is all these human beings justifying their pasts and the futures while we go about doing our philosophies. What is going to happen to these particles that dedicate lives to selling difficulty in an occult. I will spend my effort on the decision making algorithm to negate difficulty subtlely.

116

INDEPENDENT RESEARCH

Once I was driving my thought in acting smart and putting my point across in virtual reality… mathematically cuboids are slower than spheres… for having put this point across I get a question. Who is your advisor. No one in particular. If you got it wrong does not mean everything is saving the machine from ruin. Machine was formed for its own sake and not for you to show difficulty and a team effort to be recognized as the savior.

Exemplification goes only a short while and rest is independent agreement that you are as cynical as I am. I felt not to be a part of the ongoing population explosion in terms of agreement, so I remained quite in my listening and did independent research. Independent research had been a product also of independent partying. Adherence does not have enough potential that creating a story. I am OK being doing independent research than a NASA research proponent laying foundations of artificial intelligence in analysis.

117

LANGUAGE AND COMMUNICATION

People and Civilization is very very old… for to be proven in a moment. If we didn't have time to correct it till now it is a proof that a metaphysical exists. Language is often not understood. Whoever said that syllables and sounds we make out of our vocal chords is the basic structure of language. When you have negated entire representational as being something to be ununderstandable then you have reached the silence you were born with.

Our Civilization is based upon a streaming technology of communication. Why because logic cannot linearize more than the linearity of the consequential in the moment. We are embodiment and what we follow is unanimous agreement of a spectrum. That's why the extraterrestrial also as some sort of communication protocol isn't it. Can we exemplify, if we have an option of the adherential that is flowing of what is communicated to us.

118

MEDITATION AND SILENCE

Meditation is done by Yogis... let's say in the Vedic Civilization... tushnima the act of performing a ritual silently is not exact format of Meditation but is the closest approximation to what I want to say. Why because I particularly do not have adherence or an attributable to the way I leave the mind and senses open to do some sort of activity mostly for the sake of leaving the mind and senses open when my eyes are closed. When my eyes are open in Meditativeness the activity can be attributed to light.

Silence is the intelligence of the manifest in some Civilization. Silence is the light of let's say the metaphysical thought that surrounds us. It is very easy to understand the entire manifest in silence. I hope that in parallelism that we have in our Civilization we get to experience our silence from time to time. The difference between light and silence is that light manifests as a particle and silence manifests as a thought with or without time. There must be a repetitive of some fundamental thought that creates the entire volume of the thoughts in so much the same way as the Mother of vibrant mind.

119

ECONOMIC SYSTEM

Economic system must have had its origins in the lack of criticism. The essential flow and stability as well as the ease of adherence to the economic system must definitely have no redundancy. What I am trying to escape here is the capacity of criticism that can go on for a long time if we use logic to justify the economic system. I also wish that at this point I could draw a parallel between biology and economy. I console myself saying that it is there because it is there… I will think of something else… and let's say when it is not these it is not there. Civilization is very complex… more complex than the language and words to construct the understanding and the ununderstanding of Economy of Biology. The complexity of the civilization can only be addressed by the mind that subtlely understands that questioning or negating and wiping out various systems of the Civilization is not what is being asked for in most of the places. There is some intelligence to having the systems around than not having them as a consequence to human effort.

120

CRITICISM

At some point I say that criticism is logic and I need to avoid these schools of thought. After all logic is logic. When you are not a logician and have an institution some way or the other I can distantly understand that it is either analysis or criticism of the civilizational systems. Having discussed in the previous point about the inherent intelligence that is there in having systems around us… I still don't know how far I would like to be from criticizing anything for that matter. A realizable goal or may be unrealizable… I do not know as much. Hope the structure of my mind helps in my aspiration of wanting to belong to the school of thought that does not criticize much. If you know the structure of time half the job is done towards various personalities of all types is my guess on it because criticism could be a redundant function.

121

OPINIONS

Once upon a time some human beings might have had an initiative to understand how life is or even theorize. Round about the same time or even before that time there was an initiative to define the understandable. Human being can have as much opinion as it wants as long as there is a societal proof of it. Therefore, any matter of dynamic or activity must have been a failed philosophy. All the opinions are an artifact of Civilizational failures to understand.

Opinions unfortunately fall for importance. The failure often does not gain as much importance as the undeletability of a particular way of Civilizational story that can be presented carelessly. Opinions exist because we cannot undo them I guess. Still most of the Philosophy must be centered upon the already existing… that way we can be sure we have tried every which way possible to understand and that there are no more efforts to understand from arcane philosophers and importance disoriented. Civilization in quite so many ways is not going anywhere undefined or unexplored. All this is emotion.

122

REAL AND REALISM

There are two answers to what is real. All that is incomplete is real for an honest philosopher. So that it may revel upon the fact that the stationary point of everything going wrong or incorrect already is a done deal and contained in which ever manner a mistake is contained.

To answer another honest philosopher here is what I think. Everything that has a format is unreal. Tangibility is an unreal artifact of our Civilizations. Matter cannot be as honest and the surrounding often are unreal enough to create inspiration. What is real and realizable is sensitivity because it is an adherential model and what is real for the moment is Swadharma. Inspiring has to be unpersonified to a great extent and the reality has be more than whatever we already have.

123

BEAUTY AND BHAKTI

Both beauty and bhakti are Civilizational comparative study. They are abstract principles that exist in our Civilization in a funny manner. Impersonification is the key. If one wants to get inspired by beauty or bhakti one has to answer this question. If one finds anything beautiful it is not what is beautiful as much as it why you find it beautiful. Because in an adherential model there is more Philosophy on why something is beautiful. Beauty is not embodied as we think. Beautiful people don't know that they are beautiful.

Bhakti is the highest form of logic that there is in this universe. It is also beautiful. Suppose I am not making a lot of effort to understand everything and that I am not doing an importance associated activity leading to phenomenalization. Then what I say is that often times we may hit a great big wall of being 100% correct and still haven't finished it yet. Bhakti helps up in this aspect of the unfinished business of not pushing the question.

124

SOCIAL SERVICE

Let us think what is doing is to begin with. Doing is doing mostly consequence less. I have felt good examples of particles doing Swadharma or even something more personal than that. Exemplifications of individuality as difficult to speculate on are still very inspirational. I would imagine the engineer of this creation must have defined good amount of quality in centricity of our state of being.

If there exists so much quality in self what is social service is often I wondered. For a while there was mirroring to an extent of wanting to effect simplicity on to the society. Still the society often also reflects every now and then the ineffectuality of human endeavor in service... instead one would find a pattern or equilibrium or directedness of the society wanting to be serviced in a particular way. There is still a lot of idealism that has to come from the society to exemplify the efficacy of pursuing tangibility of either the society as being actual representation than letting Philosophy model society in a more Metaphysical correctness.

125

AKARMA

Akarma is like finishing it for lack of a better manner to represent the principle as sensitive. Let us see what karma is for a bit. Most of it originates from the antahkarana the individuality. Negation as a philosophical logic would not have existed if karma is nothing more than a mirror not of individual but of a premeditated adherential in time.

All Karma must exist altleast qualitatively than saying factually that things are more quantitative and Swadharma being the quality of it. How can adherence lead us to Akarma? There must have been a disconnect between individual and let's say the social dynamic. Social dynamic must be entirely an example of some sort. Still Akarma is not negation in its truth. Etymologically it must have a metaphysical representation of a stationary particle than looking at it as a definitive out of putting an a in front of it.

126

DOUBTS AND MISTAKES

Doubts and mistakes are good to have around. They help the mind to be in an equilibrium. We in a pure form cannot define everything or it may be that everything cannot define us. Therefore, we can attribute a doubt or a mistake that needs to be excluded out of our Philosophy without being too social about it.

On a closer look there is a considerable structure and pattern in either a doubt or a mistake. That although does not make it subjective or take us closer to a doubt or a mistake that exemplifying the non-stationary logic that is more alive than a doubt or a mistake. Logic also has its structure, but it is a little bit more unindividualistic than the format of a doubt or a mistake. I personally would not have an opinion on any particle looking at… or having a doubt or a mistake as long as a good communicational standard can be placed to qualify interaction.

127

EVERYTHING AND ANYTHING

I wish I could say that everything is important because I have heard someone than said that or was it their business. I do not know. Let us look at the nature of duality and draw some inspiration. Apply our minds to say what we want to say and become preferential. Once we begin to think… we may hit a stroke of deliberateness. Everything is not the same. Everything has dichotomy to it.

There is normative civilization that has its structure… it is the good part of it. Then there is this part that needs to be ignored. It depends I guess on our preferential nature as to what we want to illustrate as our gift from nature and what we feel like not spending our structured thoughts on. Language is funny. It almost makes everything subjective and flatten the entirety and present a baffling poetry. Human representation is even funnier. We have seemingly similar looking characters participating in Philosophy or war or religious fundamentalism or even just arbitrarily wandering about in some random impressionism of some arcane character of human psychology that we might as well ignore and also may be leave behind. Some time we will transcend similarity and get all qualitative.

128

CREATIONISM

Everything at some point might have been easy. Somethings might even go beyond the easiness aspect of it and occupy space and cannot be deleted even if we wanted to. Creation specifically pertaining to our Civilization I wish could have been explained for the sake of philosophical sophistication as a unified thing. The fundamental creation that we all belong to is first hand appreciation of the inverse of void space. Rest is all creationism.

Creationism must have had a separation structure from the fundamental creation in some way. The individual metaphysical particle that we carry must have some sort of a coexistential phenomenon with Geometry, Mathematics, Duality, Quantified Activity that I call a machine and our favorite artifact… Time. Once we have all this arranged in our minds nicely we can say in our philosophical simplicity that other than the manifest everything is created from scratch. Therefore, it is all pretty OK in a way to understand that most of it is not our personal business anyway and get all qualitative about life.

129

AGREEMENTS AND DISAGREEMENTS

If we see an agreement between two people, then philosophically they must be the same to quite some extent because it takes a whole lot to agree and lose individuality. Disagreements are a little bit funny because in a human space where there is no powerful artifact pushing any ununderstandability vehemently, it must be an orchestrated drama… funny for some it may be… as long as the people selling disagreements can dissociate from you every once in a while, and not ask your opinion. Without getting into it I would just say that agreements and disagreements cannot be intellectual or philosophical.

130

UNDERSTANDING AND UNUNDESRSTANDING

In an honest opinion I work hard on some aspects of this civilization. There is this part of our mind that understands things around. Not to understand is the key and that is where I help myself and others as and when necessary. It is necessary to say that our civilization and a typical state of mind of its individual already is complicated enough to represent the philosophical simplicities of other Civilizations. What it takes to understand and may be, be a part of let's say the Vedic Civilization is only simplifying.

I do not know what it takes to ununderstand anything. There is this Philosophy I can offer here that says that some of the time constructs that we experience are self-contained in the way of mimicking live human performance if you will. All is contained in the creationism of some of these experiences… everything. We can only sit back and pull Swadharma or a good quality of quality in terms of adherence. We can definitely simplify our outlook and unlearn and ununderstand up until we want to create our comfortable philosophical equilibrium of our choice.

131

VOLITION AND FREEDOM

Most of it is appreciation... we can either become one creationist can create what we want to appreciate, or we can become a part of the Vedic Civilization and appreciate the Manifest and say that the language is also a part of the Manifest. People in general need not talk about freedom or volition. Still volition and freedom exist as artifacts of nascent and preliminary forms of Philosophy.

Let me tell here what I understand of it. Most of it around here all that we like, or dislike is creationism. Some one or the other that lets say has bought the license to it creates it and does it to itself or the others. There is all the freedom in this world that needs to be put in to such people to not understand the psychology but to just say that the dynamic that we experience is nothing, but the freedom exercised by the creator of it. Volition is more interesting and what has been created can be adhered to based upon the volition. We can put a good quality of self representational in how we feel and sensitize an experiential if you will.

132

NECROMANCY

Most of my opinion of prevalent Indian from of the state of their philosophical condition is either black magic or necromancy without having strong opinions or even a second look or a second thought on the matter. If you ask me my personal definition of either black magic or necromancy I would put it across abstractly as violation of the structure of time. It is easier said than done I guess but that is the way it is. An alive participant has a sequentiality. There are somethings that cannot be done and understood by alive people. Schools of thought representing sensationalism and populism often land up selling tricks. I do not know how much of learning and personal metamorphosis these particles go through to create between themselves and any normativeness that I look for.

133

CORRECTNESS, INCORRECTNESS AND RESPECT

People and particles are of two types. Effectual people and adherential people. There is nothing absolutely correct or incorrect as they are not way too high in the list of evolved language. Topic of conversations and thoughts centered on correctness and incorrectness cannot be all that fundamental. However, for the sake of definition correctness is what an adherential person uses and incorrectness is used by an effectual person.

I do not respect people entertaining and putting up a show in more of a soft manner of eating up my time and artifact. It is difficult to say if it is all real not to mind our own business. I respect people that have a very indirect way of putting things across. More to say that there is way too much complication out there not to accept the fact and also put some of personal philosophy and a differentiation that needs to be placed as an etiquette in some communication protocols. I also respect indirect representations of people and give them all the freedom to act surprising as and when they need to.

134

CONFIGURATIONS

Everything ought to have been chaotic and a bit impersonal in our Civilization. It is to quite an extent and when it is not we begin to understand. We can understand various aspects of let's say the conspicuous… who did it… how it was done… how much do I have to understand… and at times not wanting to waste time on it. Most of the matter and life around us talk to us in their own way. Configurational is the abstract that brings anything into perspective.

We can interact with the configuration of the surroundings if you will than the components of it. This is where we can exercise a good bit of quality by bringing together what we think of the condition of any presented surrounding is. It is an intelligent way of perceiving the way of the simplicity and excluding deliberate intelligence. Intelligence has to be communicative to our qualitative volition. Human psychology to quite an extent be unsujectivised and we can still live in harmony with the surroundings without representing a great deal of change in our way of interaction with it.

135

PROOF OF BEING AND ETERNAL

Once we know that human beings alone cannot represent the entirety in our Civilization it becomes clear to us as to what we should prioritize and how to characterize a situational configuration and the exalted human that is felling like the center of the psychology. Proof of being at any level of emotion cannot be the centered human and it may be an illusion or at best represent another administered life form. Cynically speaking we need not die at all for what we do and the way it is all structured. It must be a popular belief of a preexisting before I came into being, so I will not question how much of the format we live is honest and true. Qualitatively speaking instead of talking about void spaces eternal is more talkative to us only if the pundits of our Civilization exercised more rigid control on selling their ideas. Eternal is the manifest of a form exclusive of it.

136

CONNECTS AND DISCONNECTS

Similarity is connect. Finishing is disconnect. We often think and do what we are prompted to do so we do not have to worry so much. Up until the time we feel like philosophical or simplifying everything looks in the way of a normal civilization look. We all look similar thus far… we share so many educational similarities. Educational in the sense that education and the textbook can potentially make us into clones to qualify similarity.

We all therefore must be unique discrete specimens waiting for the differentiation to come from the appropriate source. Once we feel discerned from in a definitive manner we can begin to think on the lines of connects and disconnects. We can attribute shared or common functions and attributes to a certain system that we are connected with. Philosophically if there is no need for a connect of any sort or a linguistic or intellectual inkling towards similarities then we might automatically get disconnected for better.

137

MANIFEST AND UNMANIFEST

I do not know much what an unmanifest is, but I have seen it being discussed in the Veda. So, I tried to understand that may be there is a lot more to the story than we know and that everything around us the manifest and other philosophies are not as complete and standalone specimens and will be better supported if we tell the mind that there is the unmanifest to complete the story. It is very intelligently funny.

I know more on the manifest. Manifest is something that ought to happen is the best definition. Many things around us need not happen at all. What is so special about the manifest is that in an ideal sense manifest is the entirety. It contains the individual, the surroundings, the culture, and various other sublime stationaryism that there are. Manifest is what exists along with the entity. Entity is what is not manifested… may be to create depth or may be if we stop being analytical it is the fundamental nature … the entity and the manifest.

138

ANALYSIS

Analysis is breaking it down mostly just for fun I guess. It may sound a good way to grab more words and become more talkative on various subjects. Fundamentally what analysis is, is that there are a lot of ways we waste our time. We take a meaning of a word… break the word into two and… proportionately break the meaning into two and reassign the meanings to the two newly formed fragments from the same chunk of the entire meaning. In this manner we may feel we have done something, but we essentially have not shed any light or understanding on the subject at all and the entirety of the original meaning and word have not been surpassed in any manner. Having to discuss it in more abstract terms analysis is some psychological condition that needs to be overcome in order to make any kind of progress in contributing to what I would call as the Civilizational beauty. We need to be standalone inspired candidates for one another.

139

OPTIONS AND EXERCISE

Once upon a time there was a good deal of activity and focus on decision making as an individual prerogative. I did my due diligence in dissociating with schools of thought during this process. Our Civilization for most part of it does not function on some logic like yes and no. Situations happen in a more wholesome manner. There seems to be in place something that can be exercised to be in a particular temporal configuration that we call as situation. This is called an option.

Once we are in the situation our linguistic dynamic of liking and disliking… saying a yes or a no… et cetera do not contribute towards the option that was created in its format. Any illusion of option within a particular format of our life is dishonest and unphilosophical and speculating on how it could have been better is analysis. A good experiment is to be in the idealistic environment that does not challenge our capability to put our life experiences into perspective to exercise options and present us with an option lessness.

140

INFINITY AND ABSOLUTE

From a philosophical perspective let me put forth one superlative. There is all the time in the world that you can imagine. After all that is the definition of time. The least form of evolved species of the Civilization are the ones that are like this... they have already liked the civilization and what it has to offer... they have an option to spend their lives doing the same and similar activities in every cycle of life. This format of lifeform is called infinity.

There are more evolved minds and lifeforms that say that equilibrium that is presented in the previous format is not representative of simplifications that are possible. One need not feel subjectivised to the ongoing good and the bad and participate in life like everything is one exalted experience. Everything has a structure to it and it does not make it better that its own qualitative actuality. There are these minds that simplify minds and lives to a great deal of extent and overcome philosophically time and qualify the absolute nature of let's say some sort of complacence that the civilization has to offer. We are all different in more fundamental ways than we know.

141

OPPORTUNITY AND DETERRENT

It is strange but most of our surroundings and life present themselves with a great vehemence as to signify their presence in the business from much before we ever existed. Of course, it is wrong to qualify the length in time and it has to be in the mind. Any interaction with all these well signified particles and organizations represents opportunity. There is a fair amount of importance that is characterized in social organizations and structures around us. Both people and places have existed before we came into picture. Let's say if we do not like something does it mean we have to deter ourselves from being a part of the mainstream. I would like to think that qualitatively speaking we must assign respect and intelligence to what we like… be a part of any organization that is there and imagine Parallelism and Philosophy.

142

ACTUALITIES AND PERSONIFICATION

Everybody is not the same... everything I say does not represent everybody... there are directed thoughts and comments... I need to present my Philosophy anyway. Actuality of the Civilization is this... as much as there is loads of time in the inconsequential there is infinite amount of versatility and activity of all sorts that is going on in the people and particles and unembodied bits and pieces of the society.

We cannot even fathom the unnecessary of so much in the civilization but there are always two things. Most of it is anyway happening elsewhere and society is another form of actuality that does not represent everything... it represents something... something of it may be enough... or maybe not for some people. Expressionism and personifications of being the center of original thought and activity that we may want to vehemently advertise to people around us may not be a good realizable goal. My goal is to be qualitative and simple and not criticize the social space.

143

SIMILARITIES AND DIFFERENCES

Qualitatively speaking there is a lot of verity in conclusion. This is really what I believe that as many individuals there are in this Civilization there are as many different mokshas and as many different worlds waiting for us. There is no initiative to be similar in my opinion. Inspirations have to come from a little bit more abstract and conclusive than from the fellow human being that is passing his time sitting next to us trying to pull all that similarity has to offer.

The difference lies in precedence in a fundamental manner. Similarity is like wading through duality looking for an equilibrium. I do not know what qualitative aspect can we draw of the advertised similarity and also followership represented in social flows of vehement ideologies and popularisms. Seems like similarity cannot be pushed into realism... what I mean is that if similarity exists there has to be a reason for it that I do not know that the civilizational exemplifications thus far can afford to justify. Similarity is a good research topic for people that want to do social service.

144

SELF AND MUSIC

Talking of self is talking of the manifest… manifest has embodied everything … even the language… therefore sometimes it is worthwhile to think of self and life and the manifest as some sort of music. It can be irritating to talk on self but as much as most of the irritation comes from the parochial schools of thought that use particular set of words repetitively and meaninglessly… self is also a word that has been thrown around for quite a bit to be attractive to people of all natures to be a part of some arcane celebratedness that a religious school has to offer. Bringing our focus back to addressing a more sophisticated and philosophical thought… self is an embodiment of the manifest. When we become the embodiment of the manifest we are complete. Rest is all some low level drudgery that gets glorified and proliferated calling it Quality of Life.

145

REPETITION AND SYSTEM

Qualitatively... that there is a tangible machinery in quantifying most of what is happening around is subjective to two things. Similarity and doer ship. Without either of them we would not have all the time and quality that we deserve. It is good to have similarity in this world... people around can hold on to and exemplify and feel the duality for us. Secondly is there is an enthusiastic doer that creates something for us it sets a precedence as well as defines space of discretion.

System is present, and quantification exists to a striking level of similarity and effectual participants around us. It is not that important to have it around for us. Because we get affected by the system as well as the non system. Repetition although does not happen is general for the ubiquitous goodness or the restrictiveness of the social life in general to be a fair ground of expression... but exemplification can be done. There are people that like the quantification of life in general and there are people that have duality.

146

CIVILIZATIONAL BASELINES

For most part of it, it does not matter how we get attracted to what we do as our partitioning of things we do. We work for ourselves and we work in general. Both activities are not the same but in quite so many ways we live in the same social thing and do whatever we do. One way of looking at it is that there is published or unpublished civilizational intelligence that takes away the originality out of possibly everything we do. Therefore, it is important to understand how intelligent Civilization is.

Let us exemplify that we as a Civilization coexist with other perfect civilizations in some way. That way the fundamental intelligence put into every aspect of the Civilization must bring out the effort that we do at any point. Effort can be modeled into all that we do and build upon in our lives… still there is this baseline of the Civilization that creates most of the existent in a way of not being subjective as we think to our learning or our effort. At some point however there needs to be freedom to coming out of recognizing the fact and more than getting cornered for it as highlighting religion being the basis of the Civilization… I am saying religion just as an example… it can be the man and woman thingy as well for all the intelligence we have.

147

MORALITIES AND IMPOSSIBILITIES

One incomplete conclusivity is general is a proof of completeness of various arcane aspects of the Civilization created diligently to confound and baffle us… mostly for the benefit of the numbed out observer doing as little as thinking that there is a value in attaching personal opinion and bringing things to perspective as a result of pure human initiative that how the fundamental creation if needed would have already created it if it was so necessary. Morality once subjective to human thought and linguistic skills is such a subject. Either we can be smart and distance fully develop respect for what is already there in some people or just keep efforting and find out the impossibility that is ready.

148

BLANDNESS AND PLANNEDNESS

Some people call it duality and almost start worshipping it and there are these logicists and philosophers that may consider to not put in their opinion on the subjectivity of human socio psychological busyness. Most of it was designed for some other reason very intelligent and completely elusive… but I have my own qualitative idiosyncrasies and would term most of the quantity as an un analyzed bland fuzz ball of a creation that has effectivity in some other format of presentation… and let us call it planning.

There are all these people wanting to get inspired for something or the other and the funny part is to get inspired from one thing to happen after the other or one thing to have happened before the other. We can get a little analytical and pull some quality within the event and leave the doer and the observer obsolete to have their ineffectuality. We in principle must not bring quality into life. Who knows how it is designed and for what. Only Meditation and Swadharma are distracting enough for the quantity and people around still wanting fair bit of mutual effeteness and call an opinion something else.

149

LIKES AND DISLIKES

If we have signed up not to effect people around us and do the sorts of Meditation and Swadharma… likes and dislikes are the only thing left. It is very important not to be skeptical and cynical by becoming all embracing social lover of the human conglomerate as though to have opted for this coveted place of being this equanimous example to the human populace around and to be remembered as a great value to something I do not know. I often think as to if there is all this intelligence waiting to be attributed to people around us trying to make us famous… where is the right place to attribute the intelligence.

There needed to be something astronomically natural and simple in us and around us to bring into the perspective and the righteousness to our likes and dislikes. What makes it a very important topic to simplify is the phenomenalism and memory being distributed to creating if you will unnatural examples to what can be understood as life. I believe that it is an altogether another example of how intelligence in not conclusivity of these specials.

150

SENSITIVITY AND SENSES

Senses is a good topic. We do not know what they are because we have a precedence in place to perceive anything except thought. If there is a sequentiality in place, then we are all subject to enjoying thought that has only this notion of being sensory, but this world is way too cluttered to manifest anything except reading a thought that someone has created for us. If it is very important as an antecedent to justify the life of the precedent. Once we are sensitive to value anything after negating a popular notion despite the pressure to perform we may find some interesting facts. It isn't enough finding enough to negate. What is important is focusing on the sensitive information around in various manners as much as it takes. To create equilibrium. Sensitivity and equilibrium do not come from the fact that was easy to negate and cannot be deleted. This is what most of the people sell.

151

SEQUENTIALLY

We talk about sequentiality often in presentations… what does it have to do with life or philosophy. Sequentiality is the logic that puts our intellect together. Precedence is the logic that puts our beginning together. Our mind most often looks into something is my guess… therefore there needs to be a very high level of intelligence not to distract it from this important activity of the sorts of constantly being into this something.

Sequentiality is very intelligent aspect… one of the greatest creations in time almost comparable to human quality of the words of the sorts of culture. I hope that sequentiality was created by god so that it stays in all our temporal lives. Even if I get doubtful if the format of our existence including sequentiality is created then I will philosophize a little and think we all must be a part of it or the same thing. I have one seen example of experientialism where an effect is created by altering the sequence. Unnatural it is and must not be a part of our personal Philosophy.

152

EFFECTUALITY

Often it is that the effectuality is encoded in the surroundings and not within us. This is some deep Philosophy but that is the nature of the proponents of human organizations and effectuality is more often their personal property. Anyway, for all I may say that human mind and a lot of intelligence and artifact are as still and great to exalt our looking at something Philosophy most of the time… effectuality and artifacts also exist for some reason. Very abstractly speaking it may be a part of a bad example and not independent.

Effectuality is created in one of the ways of deviating from the existing format of life. There are various formats of life and flow of time and there is one way to get it wrong and effectual for each one of it. As I said once we focus on the configuration… entire people… story… organization… presentation and the non normative effect presented is a part of a configuration. People in this configuration must be entirely creating it and sustaining it. To consider everything vital is not the goal… things exist as they exist.

153

LEARNING AND UNLEARNING

Once we have agreed upon the fact that the basic job of our mind or particle is to constantly look and almost the sort of stare into something we often can wonder about the various in effectual activities that have been around us in an intelligent equilibrium. Learning and unlearning is one of these creations. We can thing we do all we do to learn something and unlearn as the simplification as the understanding of a finer aspect may predicate. After all we do learning has to be redundified if we find something more intelligent and like manifest or like a good configuration. I hope the daily activity that we do does not reflect our learned but something more intelligent than that like some sequential order or just a high level of meaninglessness showing itself as discretized manifest once we start doing something with our mind. Some of it at least must go unnoticed and untouched by our mind in some intelligent way.

154

MENTAL DISPOSITIONS

Everything cannot be so mindful… otherwise all the fanciful and versatile individuals and their environments around would not know as to what they are doing. I hope there is some way to utter out blatantly as to who contributes what to our surroundings things and people all get very quiet and dumb if you will. Why I am saying this is that it does not take much intelligence to perceive that we all are not a particulate dispersion in a solution fighting out our ways against the evil and sorts.

Unified field theory like the one talked above is good for emotional stories but there is a lot of containment of the nature of things around us. Examples and the nonexistent take entire artifacts out of our way and put them into some sort of structures. Once we have delegated most of the clutter to configurations and structures around us we will have very minimal mental disposition to be assignable to us. Things are created using metal disposition. We may be meditators and not mentally disposed creators.

155

ALGORITHMS

Once or twice in my life I thought that someone might have done a thing or two for me to make it interesting or exiting or even to exemplify. Whenever something is done to us the usual attitude is that it must have been very very easy for the doer and must be considered as a full bodied shining illustration for ourselves in our life unmindful of the doer or their propensities. We all evolve upon a bit of awareness of the surroundings and must have been doing our due diligence to simplify actively or within.

The generic term of this nature of explicit and implicit simplification that we do is all an algorithm. I use this term because of the nature of building our perspective on the possibilities around is based on sequential experientialisms and also the stationaryness of the surroundings in the manner of a system. As things really are not going anywhere theoretically there is enough quality and intelligence that can be put in into creating our set of algorithms and see how we can improve quality of our uninteraction with the surroundings as and when necessary.

156

CONVERGENCE AND CONCLUSIVITY

I have been using all these terms out of abstract psychological propensities of simplification in an intelligent system that can afford to qualify these terms and also do a little bit more than just exemplification... something like the verity of achievable quality. Convergence as the case with geometric logic finds its way through meanings and definitions of the experiential and leave us surprisingly agreeing with a person or a fact even if we may not have a natural disposition to it. Some things are mathematical, and we can say that from the next time I will be aware of the intently. Conclusivity is a great artifact and is very difficult to find. Why I say that is that there are very very few things in life that we may come across that present conclusivity... every other form of conclusivity is our own conjecture. If life presents it in our initiative, we must feel happy.

157

MIRRORS

Mirrors is a good topic to start experientialism for various social organizations making money as well as putting a good perspective to social and individual development I guess. I am just joking but still it is a good topic to discuss in some psychological conditions. Mirror is essentially a way of accessing information from the quantities of space and time that we live in… provided we either think of ourselves as instantial or more intelligently dissociate ourselves and assign more character to the instantial and use this mirror to abstract self justified causes.

It may not need human involvement to delve into the temporal quantities of things around us. Most of the things around as much as not purely a consequence of the manifest are still mental dispositions of some sort and if I may say have a mind of its own and should be interactive in an abstract manner. Mostly for the cause of some kind of comfort in the ability to create another platform of justification for our existentialism mirror is used to thing and reflect upon the lives of individuals and configurations.

158

RITAM

Mirrors is if you will in the psychological evolution of things as they are below the nature of duality. If you understand duality mirrors is somethings that people use as an indulgence and nothing else. There is of course more stationary elements of the Civilizational quality that we live in. Ritam is above Duality. If you understand or are into the qualitative Ritam that may underlie not if all of what is around there is still some good quality of instantial that can bring Ritam into perspective.

Exemplification is of more importance than calling Ritam as Cosmic Truth. I disagree a little bit in this definition as it makes it seem like some sort of unmanifest and subjective. Ritam is a word that more like signifies the best of what we have around in this Civilization. The character of our Civilization is qualitative at even a very fundamental level and things need to be justified in either effecting Civilizational containment of some sort of an order that may have taken place to put into perspective the complexity and chaotic dispersion of quantity. This high for of justification is called Ritam.

159

PRECLUSIVE

We have defined it to have been transpondent to the observable so to have done it so many times as to have found the outward only to have considered the generic format to be distant and be solvable only when we people have not factored it into the way of centricity and also written artifacts to have been existent to being congenital to have being into it and being into it is more that the causal benefit we have running art factual surrogate to have a proponent without touching. *...and there are so many better thoughts... characterless freedom to the intelligence we live in...*

160

PRESENT

Doing is all taken into far and we have sensed it to be present… also when we have an exhibit to conform the conditional success matterful to be observed then we have not minded how things happen to not forsake the present and create presentness to be awkward not to have spoken the only way to be sensing the wave that is acting in the technology to have released all the plausibility of the pristine ness of the Civilizational intangible… and we have not felt all that needs to be felt before we get exposed to Swadharma…

We have to be open to feel all it takes to get some of the time that is spent into looking and not eat in this place as often as we listen to your opinion on whether to consider the openness being right before we have not described the freedom in a more distributed. Also we have this perception that things will fall into place with the nuancial sensitivity we have not forsaken from being overlapped shamelessly. If I were to do it, I would have not been transpiring all that has been in this worded when a certainness is attributed. We feel…

161

ANALYSIS

To have something is one with as long as we have not been together visiting this point to have more of the reflective standard as prescribed, so we all use it intermittently, so we have a point to use life in itself and be one with the progressed.

Intelligence and progression will have a way to be into us so we have not done anything so called human surface looking for otherwise and be presentable when required and also being to a thing as the processful has given into all of what we have not done to be into ourselves and be questioning the principle everyone in a while to be awake and resolve if we are there yet.

Once we had the opportunity to dawn upon ourselves with a lot of purity and we realized that if we did not do it would be another way of putting ourselves in between to make it easy so research would have taken place to satisfy our condition to be revisited. Thought will always be expressed if we have liking to the point of someone with a value. Negation is a format of consumption and take this as an example if you understand.

162

ATTIRE

All we have done is to be better in terms of not having done everything possible to support a new born into being this fortunate to have this research and also like something not too occlusive to be having a visibility to be not having done it to be a part of some art of self to be serving society and propentiated and feeling after that we have not measured the distance necessary to have not let the free to have not felt their relevance as presented with sub psycho cosmo logical as along as we felt not that we will have not efforted to be not again responding to music as a program deleted from the Opportunist for being a better genome how about that.

163

ABUNDANCE

We have not given ourselves the kind of time in to our civilization to be so active.

Often we will find things to be kind enough so the music not having taken to have the variety with a source of personal things and not active when required and then we feel so much to be fundamental into listening to some of the ways that coexist and all the way talking and doing everything for us because we are not so much a part of the inconvenient transgressions that happen to religious.

We do often take initiatives so looking forward to be not having them to be so much in the way of the character of the person involved and also being diverse and not existent where ever we go. And the points carried is taking care of them when we have not fully defined them as like you so we can be not challenged to be found at all being distributive at one or more instances characterized so we can get along with the latest original point of opulence and being there while the program fails for humanitarian reasons and we have not found the also to fit into the paradigmical if this is your own way of representing surface to having been so interesting and quiet till we have not dissected all the dislikes to be not so much equation based solution to the similarity to provide us as the basis of the quantification and looking in a certain direction as long as it takes for the reliance to dawn upon the observant and call it the latest psychological so we can elude our best or more connected to the past and feeling satisfied in one way of satisfaction that is available in abundance to call it so much to be normative waiting to be willingly performed the un analytical, also the way we only find the due characteristic of the space stimulant and feel like Chemistry is definite and Economy is best when we have not felt the difference to have listened or talked so if there are these people getting over their cruelty will always find it easy enough to have a principle to be only a part of it as long.

164

OBJECTIVITY

We have spent science with objective in a place of name to having demonstrated the value of everything, but we well wait for and answer being existent closely enough to characterize the way we have felt of the incumbent, so we have not done too much not trying to understand the point of failure.

Failure is conceived before we had things cognizant of the further, so we called upon the visible only not because we do not have any one to believe anymore in our sordid story of human way of not acting as a cell from the art.

We have felt to listen and not reflected except for our way of things in a conglomerate as opposed to being there when we want to be into it.

In the end of the day our focus on the essential is carried into time whether the NASA is looking to find an objective person to be there or just emulating the Performing Arts.

We spend time only to come across the way we preserve the naturality is suffering from explicable in the way of not letting go of the way History is constructing around the hopefulness of the Americans and the successful as long as we have not looked into our personal story to be and insightful of the God playing correct not being a part of the story but the processful defined so we can have our laughs on while we have mirrors.

Saying this is not to do it as we all have to be functional on the philosophical as we need to understand how we can be one with some objective with the point and not observe the characteristic to be the other for a while when we have not spoken to the quantifiable functional disposition for all having happened quickly.

Some of the thought may have been left behind to have everything in the spectrum of the enthusiast to have participated on the level to make us feel one of the popular ways of being there for the same value in the sequence of the oblivious meditation for having coexisted in the endurance of how you might want to be irrespective of the qualified. Time needs to be functional not adhering to descriptions that happen differently.

Quite a bit way out in the land space to have not seen people reacting other than our technical advancement and using it honestly to depict ourselves in the dream as well and we have to append time on this earth unintentful or please don't proliferate capitalism.

165

QUAINTNESS

To have found anything unclear is a matter observed as long as we have not found the interest in surrounded so as to qualify matters… we have not delved into all the histories of people contributing to the human basis but we have not point to govern the Moon as a space incentive because it is not attracting our initial effort to go as far as calculated so we can either stay or be speculative.

Quaint objects are always seen outside to not have devastated your analysis of the people that have found so many objectives at once and have calculated all to be centric.

This is quaintness is having done put in thought and analysis in front of people appreciative in general as long as we can elongate this fact of difficulty if it has happened as a center or we shall find the awkward performance to describe the way we have not been performing at that time.

The more artifacts will be eluded if the point of the perfection is a contributor instead of eating every fish that we have caught so we have not populated internet to be a format of what not has been done and that should take care of Sailors principles always so segmented to all the art as if we have not felt it…

166

VISIBILITY

We have to include this along with having everything in laughing enough of the certainty or there is a language protecting us from position in terms of the place of being conversant with or primarily we are into this vaccine called emulation as long as someone can stand in terms of speaking the same language having understandable after we have spoken.

Things will get visible as long as multitude does not represent an alternative to a better way of presenting our forgiveful life of the purpose we solve one at a time so in case we got some inspiration from the spiritual it can be stretched.

Along with this cognizant of the personification we have so many people only a deterrent on the Vedic way of delivering our duties only in this subliminal cosmological event thinking that they could be better described in music than our effort.

In case you wondered as where we have not made progress to have everything aligned for only warring Sailors sentient with all it takes in terms of description we have to make ourselves so to be recipient of the visible.

The only plausible is to remember well if we have been constructing this thought of the only explicable like a wayward for all I care of the glorious years of emulating in research.

167

LOVE

I will miss this mistake fortunately talked into something that has happened in spite of the hard art that has been the only way of being parallel not felt the point of being in there for being for something evading the science of the most intelligent to begin with to have caused it to have this benefit of not trying another language for being so concordant with all the participle will take place to do me most of my work.

We will have this for not having started on this directive of dancing too much to have emulated rockets and it is not my mistake to tell them as to how it can be once we have taken one and the other for the sake of society. Meanwhile we are trying not to get back at all.

So if we have called this inexplicable happening it must have been done to make its way into all the possible ways we can interpret all the ways we have been looked upon to have distorted the conception of this fact that people are to be born only into a hemispherical laden upon meaning than the contribution that love may have one day to talk more freely than the minister.

I love we have not felt how we have been different so let us be objective as positioned along the recipient of the fallacial American response to being so not thinking this fact you not have overridden the continuity progressing as we talk on unsubjective while we have paralleled ourselves on our capacity to being unobservant particle only closer as a way of being incentivized for not having not presented this way of interpreting all the work we will do to always generalize the way of the possibility of thought to have taken place so we have not found an Opportunist finding a useful information to be drunk enough…

168

NATURE

Light is a form collecting to be continuous if substance is felt as perceptive at once. Behavioral is not something to have occurred to take a content off it for having said that we have boxed cognitive.

It will present some part of the unmindful to the responsive and not to prove logic as we perceive in a sense also evolving to make it effortful. In time some of the linearity is to have definitional consequence to fulfil the human condition may be a number of times.

Question is geometric to be incomplete or instinctive is being evolved as we have intermittent objects as told to un perceive. Why would it be complicated to have coexisted is looking for a reason along with qualification of juxtaposition for not personifying existence as communicative. We can do it mathematically provided the development is to happen equally in senses not interfering with time as being taken place also for example.

169

COHESION

We have something to do with the place and also, we need inside not consisting all the factual as the other person did in the same place. What do you call the point when we have not felt the incumbent to have asked a question?

Theoretical point gets it from another point and the consistent is distance for the time being of the way it is but not mirrorful as we need to be unthoughtful to have lived through it as getting appreciated to be recognized is not the point to have taken place at all and we have time to define effort.

Cohesion is not a failure is what a philosopher would say as long as it is almost perfect to have taken place for the consistent negation as acceptable of for letting it sink in defining itself when we have not done it. All we can say is to be valued for all that takes place between time and the consistent leaving coherence behind is an example to define also. Sense has to be expressed is a connotation and the subtlety will be attributed. Conversational is consistent with light.

III

STATE OF TODAY

170

GOVERNENCE

The realism necessary in theological study is one that is time consuming. The surroundings with initiatives in this context are mostly controlled as policy. Everything has a source but not quite as tangible given that the history involved differs from ministry to let's say culture.

Whether government is asking for attention to bring value is a constraint and needs to be addressed first even before we feel free to define a project to be conservative as a research should be. It is difficult initially to go about communicating among our people involved given the expectation that is sensed.

I believe that ministry and establishment get first priority and we need to outline programs to focus on deliverables that may be implicit. We may have to talk with ourselves and see how far a study can go without digressing and losing interest to imposed.

So, having established a rapport with recent history of our setting, we need to think metaphysics. Surely, we will see how to successfully transition our effort and effectively portion our original ideas with what is beneficial to all.

Seems a bit socialistic but will be able to bring into perspective the vastness of what this civilization has in terms of human value. Cultural sentiment is one of the central themes. Original research or original idea may have to find objectivity in appropriately representing the historical promise.

It may be a good topic in itself that idea will survive reality. Philology is a good example of many great minds have stressed on the ways of rigid research. Nothing we can negate but depth of the subjects may not be apparent and will be time consuming without expertise.

There is a lot to learn from experience of an institution and respect is involved. The cohesion of this magnitude is spectacular. Individuality will surface. Competing with technological and scientific innovation will bring its own direction and we have the beauty of speculative philosophy to consult with. It is truly rewarding as an experience and to be a part of.

Our existence is also cluttered with some mistakes and failures, but we will have time for all. Some like inclusive commentaries and religious experience. Some prefer silence and belief. It is not sure where we will land in all the effort vested.

Surely religious study will need a parallel because it is so different from rest of the subjects. I am hopeful of successfully bridging the gaps keeping the openness of the mind. People will bring impulsive psychology and interpretation. We need to see all the structured research and thought also. MTS program and the school will redefine future research and personal interests. Overall, I will feel how to contribute to our civilization. This study will have the reward of the world peace and global humanitarian value. And I will be able to express our complexity beautifully and religiously.

171

EVOLUTION

Let us start this with time. Putting across all the thought must have required a structured mind. But structure is limited so we cannot begin with too much of it. Is there some value in unstructured when we think vastly? Definitely the answer is yes but not so straight forward.

This is probably the reason for chaos. Theoretically there is not much difference between time and chaos. Analytics will show that there is something we like about both these artefacts of our existentialism. Something we like must have been created from chaos or time.

Now if we think abstractly we do not have either time or chaos at hand. All there is around us is consume form of life. So, we do not have time at hand. We cannot reach the necessary condition to treat ourselves as complete or the limit.

So, agreement on time makes us come to the limit. Concluding that the limit of our life is not imposed by time, so we cannot dissolve our life. So, we get emotional and start to say that at least we will value. This is an important point.

Emotion plays an important role in a religious frame of mind. All this that starts from here is negative or negated. We can actually not differentiate between religion and emotion as we in our life adhere to essential and can do it all the way.

Adherence is called dharma. All of our sentiment is beautifully described using abstract definitions and language. This is the point where individual can be more or less successful. This is where the story begins. I hope when we lose adherence and talk quality of life we are not regressing culture to be equal to us mentally or geometrically.

What does it take to start talking about life and complete a circle? When we buy things, we need to be aware that circular thoughts are what we can value when talking philosophy. We call it expertise to start talking in circles. We can imagine what we are subjected to.

Life is a parallel to expertise that exists at any given point. We have to understand how much there is metaphysically and how much we can witness the creation of the point. Creation in its entirety is in form of an understandable example. Life goes on as we pay attention to this tendency.

So, we cannot see if someone is having a metaphysical attempt to present us how it might have been. We will like the thought or reject it depending on which ever increases our value. So, all of the philosophical fervor keeps being into our life's, thoughts and minds from all over the place.

We at this point can say that in the midst of life we have the individual's boundary and constituents.

172

SUCCESS

There are some topics like the unknown, communication, personality stereotypes, beginning etc. that surface when we attempt to define definitively the objectivity and purpose of life. It is theoretically not possible to not be a part of some form of existing ideology.

We will try to define some subjectivity and make our circles around just being communicative in a good way. It becomes important to make individuality work to a very high level before we feel incumbent to some generality. It is called making things work their way out.

The essential point to begin is to contribute to self and there is not much biologically defined to feel like a specie with an example. There have been institutions that successfully launched people in the correct metaphysical to find individual basis and religious account.

Exemplification is the most difficult to differentiate ourselves from. Science is primitive and cannot satisfy the inclusion without complicating anything. It is good to see examples that we are a part of including our lives conclude and make us effective in enhancing the personal gap.

Typically, ritual takes from where our example concluded. Not everybody is as similar. We must know how it is structured. We must be able to establish quality limits and sufficiency to say what we are achieving. We must define value without consuming life.

Observation analysis is the most important. We generally associate philosophical conditions and the exclusive intellectualism with some quietness associated with being an observer in life. The problem is the active form of our splendid life is on the background while we are wasting time.

It is very difficult to say why some tacit points have been put into experience as an observer. We cannot negate that there is some simplicity associated with this theory, but it does not predict our intelligence. Intelligent people are more peaceful and aware to the light of life.

A lot of people and a lot of effort does not quite inundate intelligence in spite of the interference. Objectively there is a lot of redundant structure surrounding us no matter what we do. Expecting is imposed to make somethings work for no big reason.

There are so many parallels to people and life being not concrete and being fuzzy. Life is emulated cheaply and effectively. Quantitative reasoning is arbitrary. Abstraction is necessary not to indulge in competition. Doing things and following principles is silent. Once again there is quite a large volume of life that is just imposed and just goes on. There is not much value in retrospect.

173

SOCIAL

Sometimes we get to doing things unplanned hoping to equal intellectual performance of the past. All human endeavors have been preserved as fossils. So, by getting into the history of things we can expect to outlive them. Religious study must have a good beginning template so one can act smart just on subjective.

We have taken a sarcastic note when we came to history is the truth from my personal opinion. I like to see as much being squandered as an institution can push. This is probably a planned consumption behavior expected by ancient researchers. In this context history is important as we at a very high level are into the business of appreciation.

Inquisitive and instinctive research is the successful outcome of the way some talking culture has evolved. I will just say here what comes out of culture stays in culture. I feel the most treasured artefacts get represented in history as exemplificative or experiential not worried with intellectual property because it is way too smart and limited.

Also, I feel the only kind of approach to religious and cultural exposure is not cognitive but competitive. This is called studying things using history. When we start to express or communicate our research, we understand that we are not presenting history, but we are competing. Anyway, there are various possible studies and realisms.

Research in its working form is being done by people that have considerably strong aptitude. We are not talking the popular research community and how they commercially dig out stones. Also, we have research as an avocation. Interestingly some topics are covered and represented historically almost celebrative active concepts. So, what is an active subject.

Models of individuality and funny part of yourself is represented in spheres. The most subtle concepts of social objective and religious emotion is represented in counting. This is called historical perspective. I try to put objectivity to giving complete definitions to this part of the study. In general, it is all our history but gets into the levels of self realization.

I have also studied science from this historical approach putting people in their place and respect. There are things disclosed and some are tacit. It could have been my original idea but generally attributed to general history. Also, history is quite far a stellar object not reached by policy and governance. Good for us the pristine.

It is good to see how much is contained in naturalism that is not regulated. Not too much to find people sustaining what it takes to set things apart. This is very important to have continuum of unsuccessful and economy. From duality perspective we can define a parallel life form not in only one but for several occasions. So, the question is does success also gets sustained or all historical approaches are original beauties. Definitely some people are dispersed like stars in the sky.

174

RELEVANCE OF HUMAN PARTICIPATION

There is a sphere for mind and there is one for body. And there were socialites that took this sublime concept and popularized it among the undeserving. Spheres are of course everywhere. Common people used mathematical representations that made them compete with the rich. There is one thing that is not represented spherically and that is communication.

So, what is the difference between spheres and circles. Circles are representation of existences in schools of thoughts. Often consuming all the framework described in talks. Spheres are not like anything circular. When we use our body to exemplify our involvement in an incident we use a spherical representation. Spheres represent complex geometric information to have a form of completeness, so we never talk this that what is outside of a sphere.

Spherical containment of mental representation of concept of involvement of things happening in accordance with certain example. Up until a long time various examples evolved to say that life is like this or like that. Beautiful speculative philosophy used spheres to contain human experience. The concepts with spheres became so popular that people in ancient world made un fathomed progress in metaphysical.

The current state however is to delegate an entire type of human beings to the juggling they can do with spheres. It is very sad to part with spheres, but it is ok to have low levels of existence handle concepts carelessly. Some rift must have caused this commercialization of spherical concepts but as with low levels the destination of people misusing concepts is unclear.

The problem is that subjective ideas of our life are realizable in spherical or dream concepts but as with anything a good concept has a home and we must know where it belongs unlike the distribution of wealth in opportunism. Mental concepts became to be rampantly used not as a solution to problems but just because we began to count people.

In religion and related experience, it is derogatory to socialize concepts involving simplicity. The good part of the story is that the destructive power associated with spheres is very high, well researched, and imminent to not worry about the distribution that happened because of war or media. Secondary and associated ideas are everywhere, and we need not expose ourselves and experience negation or an example of what not to do these days.

People can talk for you and I do not know what sort of countries and governments commercialized religion. Before the wars time was at hand and value of human sort could be felt over long periods as necessary to adhere to our principles and evaluation.

If there is any time to celebrate simplicity it is the post war period as we can feel all the good that was consumed in our civilization in our history. We will definitely find exclusive organizations and establishments going about living complex life ideas administered in dreams in spherical.

175

INCOMPLETENESS

Ineptitude is to be set free. Some of the psychology never makes it. Number of people must not pretend in a country. We still have not seen the outcome of sociology, opportunism and democracy. Doctrines are only current technology and there is not much basis to having a social moral objective. It is very important as an irreligion strategy to let things happen and if we are smart accelerate.

There is not much more than completeness of anything that is confusing. We have to agree that our civilization still is a sacrificial model unless the socialistic promise is recorded and kicked into practices. What is the similarity among communication, definition and numbers. They all have an inherent negation and cannot be a part of religious performance.

What is outside is what is inside because we have left number of people taking it for free and emanating thought. The thought that once had risen the man to self realization. One such thought is the theory of numbers. We must have regressed when we asked ourselves what the minimum number is when we take the initiative or thought of counting ourselves.

We really have to think where the stationary point is when we have a cumulative order disorder. Thought has never been cumulative, and our originality is competing with government policy. I wonder who is making money out of policy. Anyway, without digression we must admit to the fact that civilizations that evolved on birth and death must have had basis of number theory for counting ourselves and the necessity of this activity to be justified to be brought into existence.

We can build a brand new country or invent a good civilization that lives life instead of using communication as education. We need to segregate all the subjective that is just talk. There are number of minimum tendency philosophies. But it can only move forward and create an exclusive community that promising annihilation.

Great annihilation is never going to happen, and we need to commit to ourselves the only necessitated and make it a part of our religion. What does this mean. Religion is not a commodity to let people feel similar. We cannot rule in democracy as a principle. All that is existing is negated in exemplification. And if we want to have a metric not to revel in people and multitude we need to find out that thought is longer than life.

Success is vested in anything but the original. Path of realization is slow and is open to comparative study only after we have thought a lot of correct thoughts. Once we enter the regime of comparative philosophy we might as well become a bit sarcastic for all the unfounded people that embody something that you don't.

Richness has always been in a necessitated condition and we still need to quietly observe people that have separated from involvement of pop music. There is not much in music and propaganda than finding oneself not enjoying it for a correct reason.

176

ANTHROPOLOGY AND RELIGION

Concept of minimal activity leads to religion. Ritual is an activity set aside from colloquy. Introspection is prayer. The center to set aside the value of something as consuming time is a silent disposition. We need to understand a few concepts. Centricity, value, silence, and disposition. We all have a decent bit of exposure to religion in more than one way.

We need to begin religious study as just in the nuance of being or having exposed to something as it fits into the normal substrate of what we live. So, religion is a kind of exposure. And correlated function that we call prayer is definition of religion. Prayers reach the levels of silence that are required to bring out what is hidden in silence of the religion.

Actually, if we pay a close attention religion from any part of our civilization is not a verbose written statement. Terse forms of communication and expression that exist in religion to be preserved. There is not a special initiative that any religious activity in our history has to set it apart and be alive if for example we set it to compete with economy or a scientific or psychological experiment.

Our disposition into silence of religion is often destructive. Religion is not quite fortified to not include participation. Religion can be completely redefined. Prayer is the part of religion that is carved in stone. As we see that prayers have their own disposition and are included in religion to give us an extra sensory perception.

What is it that we need to include or exclude is that disposition of personal nature is expressed in every moment of our life. We cannot bring our disposition into something because it is a separate entity. The value of prayer is as big as quantified individual performance. If we understand the nature of prayer, we will definitely know where we are free to perform.

Is a prayer dissuasive of changes? Why does it have a personage? We are people that have expressed volition at every moment of our life. We have created things and invented communication to create around us what we live in. We have used metaphysics to have a business. We have commercialized nature. We take examples of naturalism and invent ways to advance.

What we typically know as a research initiative and the outcome to be advancement of the human or our civilization has a lot vested. So, prayer is not a part of our progress. Prayers create a sense of accomplishment. Do we know what exactly is accomplishment hidden in a prayer? I am sure some psychological organizations emulate prayers at a very high level to invent forms of existence.

Study of prayers is a great research topic, but I am not sure how to begin. That is the good part of being an accomplished prayer. We have set prayer as a parallel without the incentivized part of our existence. We have schools that make us define principles to make everything we do as being an incentive driven process. Prayer is different. We may argue what we do vehemently is like a prayer. Prayer is set apart from the person praying because we do not know what we do.

177

PURPOSE

Life is an opportunity. Value is psychological. We need to pass through things with a certain ease. Some theories as ritual only make sense when we encompass it. We are in a civilization that is somewhat rich in religion. Across the globe the top most avocation is religion. Having said that we need to see how we got introduced to the concept of ritual.

We all in some way or the other have learned to be a part of social activity. We definitely know what a social function is. We can call it a ritual. Because of gratitude we need to continue doing things as we see from long time back and keep doing it ritualistically for very far. We have something at hand that we need to appreciate.

There are two perspectives to ritual. We know we have been a part of something psychologically when we witness almost after the event of what can be termed as nuance of self realization. From there we draw a parallel of similarity and get hooked to a psychological being almost reminded often how we stumbled such a realization.

It is great to have first self realization, and it is almost the way of nature to start or initiate upon a ritual to signify such a thing to have happened to us. Next is how did we ever stumble on this opportunity. There is some religious propensity that distinguishes among people as self realized and not. We need to see how socialites flaunt opportunity.

Ritual is where the mistake also is. So, there is a demarking in ritual making it more personal than a social function. I can go on tagging ritual to an opportunistic event of self realization than just a mere social function for more than one reason. But it does not work like that. To push an idea is not the direction of the social.

We have witnessed ourselves to be in psychology when it comes to religion, prayer, ritual, function etc. Associatively our psychological disposition is interfered with by getting something out of it. We need to know how to differentiate the entertainment value out of somethings. We can stop empathizing with the source of ritual or realization.

According to media, there is always a person or an organization that is original point of supporting the ritual. I have not been able to overcome their vehemence to popularize their presence in our life pretending to be making a profit out of our opportunity of realizing one's self and embracing the ritual. In all the event that happens to us like a light needs to disperse into space and not into commercial value.

There must have been more religious civilizations that center life around ritual. Vedic civilization is definitely one of those that need to be differentiated from our civilization and studied to understand existence in its form as an existence and not a belief. This is one of the most important point is if complete definition of life is not our mental conjecture. It will take a long time to understand this.

178

SPACE

Most of the religious subjects are devoid of human experience is my observation. We have various versions of human involvement and commitment in connection with religion. In such a context we are not really creating a human centric experience and commercializing it. Truly religion is an inundating experience in itself.

Having distanced human drama from religion it is a good place to talk on the subject of peace or the Sanskrit word for it, shanti. We clearly need to distinguish our personal necessity to be at peace with one's self and the metaphysical peace. When we involve ourselves and our surrounding in a religious stand point be it a ritual or prayer, we definitely invoke a lot of elements.

Actually, religious ceremonies are made out of elements in our nature and psychology. That is the realism involved so we know we are doing a religious activity and not just a human interaction. So, what are these elements that participate with us in a religious function. Wind, Water, Earth, Fire and Space. We need to be sure what the definition of each of them is.

Apart from the elemental involvements in a function we involve ourselves at various levels. We involve our Self, Speech, Action into our religious prayer. We also do something with diligence. We use all these aspects and energize the atmosphere as necessary depending on the typical nature of function we are doing.

There are a lot of various functions and their purpose. We interact with all the presented and defined aspects and receive our gift from the ceremony. Having involved all these aspects created a religious commotion. We need to be aware of this. And towards the conclusion we let go of each of these aspects to their default state. This is the fundamental process of peace or shanti.

We remind ourselves having interacted with nature and self at all levels possible. We express our sense of gratitude, and appreciation to all the constituents present in the function. It is very necessary to restore peace at all levels as the interactions do have a certain effect on us and surroundings.

We can take this general idea of peace from our religion and put into practice in rest of the places as well. We need to increase our awareness in the activities we do and the people we interact with. We need to help people in their agitated state of life. We need to propagate the inner peace and normativeness to our friends.

Human race is always on the move. There are a lot of people doing a lot of things in all sorts of ways of freedom. Freedom leads to human competition. People get energized and say and do a lot of things. We need to take initiatives to understand others and make it a point to help people in need because their suffering is caused by us only in an indirect way. We have to make it a point to spread the word of peace at the end of every interaction or activity and maintain equilibrium.

179

NEGATION

In philosophy the most beautiful thing is negation. To understand what negation is takes a bit of reading and training. Mostly the language we use in modern world itself has an implicit negation. History is different. Historical text usually uses topics that need textual negation.

Favorite historical topics are Truth, Knowledge, Abundance and Quantity, Creation etc. All these topics are studied in contextual negation. For example, we may present something as false and negate it to fortify the truth. We keep on adding text and examples of what is not true and get the required time and fuzzy definition of the philosophical truth.

In philosophy also, nature is not this actual biological nature. When we say nature in philosophy it means metaphysical quantity of a topic such as goodness. We all know what we do not like. So, there must be a place devoid of such things. This is called true nature. Natural goodness is what we all belong to. We can give it a name or just keep fortifying it with arguments.

This quantity of time and text and the related study has the name neti neti. Literally neti means this is not it. The subject could be anything we like. Most of the ancient knowledge fortunately covers the things we psychologically like. This makes the text and connected religion attractive.

In our modern world we have advanced this topical negation to not only the things we like but also other examples. The examples and stories collected in one place could cover a topic such as causality. It is the most complicated topic in the history of mankind. We neither scientifically nor philosophically know anything of the nature of cause and effect.

Our story must include somebody doing something like a call and watch for a response. Then we say that the probability of response must have been driven by something like a coincidence. Thus, causality has been negated leading to finer details required to attribute our complex existence.

So, negation has its root in complexity. Our ability to distinguish unsatisfied condition is the center of this entirety. It makes it easy to say that if the quantity associated with dissatisfaction is so much in number, then the satisfied condition must also exist in vast quantities as well.

Thus, religion is directly connected with large quantities of something. We cannot however say than negation belongs to religion. Religion must contain the outcome or the conclusion of negation and not the effort and the process involved.

What is the outcome of a lot of examples and stories is that we might think the complexity is dispersed over time. Time for sure takes a form of negation and presents a parallel to religion. I say this only being hopeful that we have incorporated the required quantity of respect and not leaving any doubt in the rigidity of what religion is.

180

HISTORY

I feel there are a lot of things we do according to our aptitude. From this point it is easy to take a historical attempt to find what it takes to create a story. We have spent vehemence in adage or daily thought. We have founded our justification as a new subject. Often times we may hit upon original ideas that seem to be appropriate to our talent that is speaking for itself.

I do not want to ascertain that this preoccupation with talent oriented performance and all the data that comes from being active in research as a human in modern society. It is well known that most of what we have at hand is intelligently crafted but not coherent enough. How do we avoid this tendency to be popular?

I think that subjectivity is well founded. I will avoid tendency. Research or thought that takes into account the notion of self representation go on unhindered. Apart from this promise of being contemporary, I feel to take an historical approach to the matter. People need to be studied from the time when subjects were not manipulated.

But the amount of intelligence represented in a particular subject an only last as big as the circle is. We have to be used to latency. What it means is that there is an entire pattern that has more subjective imprint by considering all subjects as all pervasive in time a geography.

Referring people with orientations is what historical perspective is. We might think the kind of time we spend on subjects is advanced culture, but our lives are still in the solvable territory. There is not enough matter built up in our imagination to say we want to reinvent.

Even scientific thought or theory is dependent on what we can communicate. So, if communicating is all we are doing where do we find the matter that relates well with any subject. The sooner we realize the communicative form of our psychological propensity the better it is to consider ourselves as just a proponent of the existing.

So, if all the cumulative advantage we have living in modern culture is additive in nature, we might become just a historian trying to say this is where we began creating a story. This is the exact point where our talent and intelligence took the frivolity turn to consider that with our creativity we have been able to study and also create a story.

I am sure we can altogether avoid the story of science or even history if we become cognitive of what is more important. The creative part of our research always does not represent how we want to adhere to the story of science or religion.

We have to consider that it is not important to the person envisioning a story of history to be understood as poetic or a condition we call as liberal at our time not being able to understand.

181

IMPORTANCE OF MINDFUL CREATION

We are not only witnessing history from a psychological perspective, but we are liberating thought not at our end but uncertainly thinking optimal and suboptimal creations of human backlog. When do we embrace a topic is known to the person who did it.

Subjective and personage are very important when we start enjoying what we do. The attempt to build a story could not have gone far to engage intelligent people. In essence once consumed the subject can only be revived historically.

People have been creative to find one instance in thought and the other in practical application. Not that practicality is easier that thought. Because we do an experiment willfully. What does all this skepticism mean. We just cannot create an opinion in a domain.

Most of the research and even our lives were not promising to research. People of all types did what they could as society permitted. I sometimes feel that the concept of genius or a respective domain expertise was not well founded for us to take on subjects without finding random people just contributing to the story.

It is very important to find people inundated in beginning of the theology than contributing to it. As it is easy to define a story and create a mental makeup. And we don't even have enough to say that only the most intelligent survived.

We can only be as commercial in our research orientation. It is not unimportant to be understanding. But it is easy to catch one person creating a story because of lack of data. There was a time when data was all we generated. But to talk on data is being referring to high levels of honesty we may not be a part of.

Higher levels of human conjectures will have to recreate the magic. Historical approach neither adheres nor creates. The most effective is to find a historian talking whether creating a subjective is natural enough to follow a path. I think that originality has something to do with the beginning philosophy.

The better we know exactly how much time to spend in the beginning and how much to delegate to the under intelligent to survive on our thought is not as entertaining. People have had the time to do what they wanted to do in a more articulate form than our story of success.

We will find what drives life if we forgive ourselves to be a part of someone else's creativity. We need to get into the verity of the subject not as described by the people. Associative is not the essence of creation. The origin of subjective thought and if possible adherence to all that is created from the history of thought. I wish there was another definition of the beauty in original and adhere to it.

182

POPULAR BELIEFS

Belief is the heart of civilization. What is more relevant as understood is popularity. So, let us think what would be the shape of popular belief in our system. Community fervor is conveyed as popularity. The most difficult part of our civilization in surroundedness. Almost all of human mental process shapes up as having been inundated in time.

Inundating belief in time is a very difficult task. We are mostly colloquial intelligence. Things as present are just a matter of circulated effort from our side. Any output in terms of study or research mostly comes to becoming a belief just because everybody is talking similarly.

Similarity in cultures and celebrative psychology creates its own circles. What is more interesting is that we will find it difficult to attribute realism to popularity. The way it simply works is that one finds to be centered with people being in unanimity of any belief.

It is not sure why we have popularity and celebrative attitude to be a part of religion. It does not have the required intelligence more than just being all around. Can we distinguish a religious concept from a popular belief? People go as far to say that the basis of religion is a few numbers of popular beliefs.

How much effort does it take to define a set of stories and circulate them in time. Over a period, the story becomes a part of our belief system. It again is a social activity to sustain or even discard any thing from popularity. It is very interesting to find patterns in the kind of stories that are around us. Also, it is built in into popularity not to compete.

Competition brings about the subject of intelligence and brings a sense of difficulty to our race. Thus, when we associate ourselves to what is being popular or circulated we cannot debate on the topic more than how anything is defined. It is only one layer of language that supports easy philosophy.

We can base our argument at this point to say that we need to be able to say what business we are into. Civilization may be teaming with enthusiasm with a set of popular beliefs while we have secluded people researching the intelligent aspects of our life.

Schools of thought exist for both popular belief systems as well as the contrary intelligent behavior supported by very few. Intelligent concepts are structured differently from popularisms. Language is used in a different manner to preserve intelligent parts of our religion. We can associate more practicality to intelligent beliefs. Human initiative is not the one that is sustaining the heart of the matter.

Most of religious fervor is rooted not in the easy and popular belief systems. Intelligence brings about a lot of vehemence to religion that is difficult to understand but must be addressed.

183

LANGUAGE

If we are able to understand geometry and language we can create a good story. In other words, language and geometry do not have anything in common. They are so disparate that the most complex parts of our lives are essentially constructed using language and geometry.

Deterministic examples of our life are nothing nut attempts by human beings to understand life using language and geometry as emulating a particular concept we are trying to understand in our life. But having said what exists around us as being a complex created out of geometry and language, we also have geometric concepts devoid of language and vice versa.

It is very important to limit ourselves when we are talking about attempts by humans to explain or understand life. Not everything is poetic and made to be simple and enjoyable. We have no way of containing the volumes of stories using language and figures.

There is an entire research to be present to understand what human output is. We need to be able to contain the amount of theory. Pure form of geometry is essentially a dream. Similarly, pure form of language is coexistence. In a more metaphysical manner language has its own life and sustains what it contains without human activity.

Language with its parallelism to our life holds the key to poetry. People have defined great details of appreciation in language. So, one may wonder why is not there more of the appreciative from of linguistic fervor. It could have been very simple according to me is we did not stress on similarity in life concepts.

The beauty of language is that it does not contain effort. But there are various types of expression that tell us a lot of diverse human saga. Again, I believe language is exclusive to making us try to understand life.

Religious rituals are described using pure forms of linguistic expressions. We can almost find our when exactly in our civilization we began to go wrong. There is not much in our civilization that can be undone but it is good to have rituals and poetry expressing the appreciative part of ourselves.

Once we start to express appreciation of let's say nature or even human nature in language we will see how independent language is to consider everyone treating us individualistically. What it means is that there is not much restriction in how many people start to appreciate life and express it using language.

It is interesting to see how poetry evolves almost describing the same beauty over and again in different times and by different people. It is fortunate to have good language and desire to express the finer aspects of our life using language.

184

NUANCE

Most of what we have around us is qualified in two ways. First, we all do have quite a lot of mental capacitated life to put forth quantities of happening. And happening is easy to create as well leading to volumes of time and data.

Governance in modern days can be summarized as a sensory program. All we have at hand is quite a lot of theories slowly being present and presented irrespective. There are number of people and a number of attempts to all the possibilities of what life is. Does anyone get it or get it correctly is a different subject altogether? What is needed to think on what theories explain our civilization to the required complexity.

When we have enough complex attempts to describe life and think we want to change our topic a bit, we start theorizing simpler explanations. We have adage to supplement our failure. Anyway, the outcome of initial thought on what is going on around is undeniable failure to explain what life is and there is all the incentive to give it another attempt.

The goodness of our humanity is nothing but incentive to create another sensory conceptualization. This is where we do not know if for sure all our systems are able to be evaluating the correctness. Difficulty in getting things correct is also an incentive to go wrong.

Having described everything as an intellectual attempt we can see what survives in the in spite of condition. The correctness and the right things are a little more subtle. To complement our behavior religion and ritual must have been existing in nuance.

What it means is that quite a lot of sensitivity is required to understand quite a lot of things covered in religion. We can be very hard faceted about astronomy and reveal all the sectors of the moon. Is it quite possible to do that? Not quite a deterrent but just a nuance.

Similarly, there exist various facets of our mind and psychology. We still have not been able to analyze the difference between an incentive and what we like. Nature exists around us in sorts of ways that can be described almost as being elusive, but the reality is that it is also subtle.

The sooner we realize what it takes to create a good parallel to our emotion not to override the correct conjectures that don't quite go a long way to support our incorrect behavior. Nature is definitely not elusive to understanding. It is just that lot of things happen as a part of governance and incentive that do not hold the promise to describe the finer things in life.

Actually, the structure of life itself is inconclusive. We can construct enough life activities and arbitrary conclusive events in our life and keep the actuals facets of interactions of the other kind.

185

REDUNDANT EXPRESSIONS

Redundancy and respect correlate our avocation to understand religion.

We seem to have a lot of unobjective talent to keep doing things and not call ourselves into being redundant give ourselves a conclusivity. We may choose not to create stories and conclude our activities in life and not contribute to generic format of conjecture.

Studies must reveal that activities that happen to us are not quite correlateable to our deservingness but are rooted in certain random function. For as far as I can see we can delude ourselves to calling randomness as being characteristic of life.

Rich countries definitely have good programs to sustain research in various areas of science, psychology, religion etc. While the rest of the world is celebrating mediocrity to the limit to what can be a government subject. It is difficult to name what is uncommon.

Correct initiatives and research projects in our world seem secretive not because there is true value that cannot be distributed to everybody for free. Incentives work differently. Correctness is inconclusive and does not reward humans.

But good research must go on without justifying the time and effort spent not quite giving us another movie to watch or another emotional drama we celebrate in our mediocrity. It is not too hard to notice that most of what occupies the space in our world is tolerance to redundant format of explicable existence.

Incentives and human talent are not existent everywhere. Our research and study are mostly middle level just occupying time and generic disperse of activity and economy. Great researches may not tell the actual story.

Correct formats and conjectures are better derided than being a part of our lives and the world in general as the experiments in our formats separate humans in a definitive and different manner. There is not much in what is said or done.

There has to be other bodies than ministry trying to create fundamentality in the art of creating a story that becomes successful in masking the actual problems that get celebrated in ordinary world. There is quite to be done not to expose mediocrity to people.

Countries and policies must do what they feel in their format of freedom and reach levels of where it becomes a natural separation of our story of incentive and redundant growth and the correctness a being an altogether different specie available to only the deserving.

186

CIRCULAR CONSTRUCTS

The most important in education of philosophy is trying to understand a line and a circle. Linearity is the outcome of living life in a sequence. Circularity is a mental construct. I think we just understand a circle from the geometric perspective and impose it with thought to make our understanding easy.

We all experience life in events. We all have felt how events in life have a semblance to what is probably a humanly created artefact. It is sometimes worthwhile to recognize what actually is life or a part of our life and what is creation.

A lot of thought in modern society gets created. It is nothing except for creation. Creating anything uses ingredients. There is something we all understand. And there are things that get accepted just the way they are.

Due to extreme competition in understanding life and doing something philosophical some schools of thought started creating thought constructs that can be experienced. They get administered in our own process as something like a dream.

Some schools of thought consider administering thought constructs as a part of educating people and accepting them in a particular way of a group of people thinking alike.

The point is when a thought construct gets created and administered as education or a dream, there needs to be a way of saying what we want to achieve by doing such a thing. Creating anything mentally is actually creating it out of nothing.

The matter in thoughts may be superimposed on a certain circular format. Circular formats represent a way we all reason out things. Because circle has completion inbuilt. We can start with any argument, and fragment in in beginning and ending. We can also fragment it a cause and effect.

Another way to fragment thoughts is how we become protective of the goodness in life. Something like a story, creating a sense of being heroic in taking the good part. How we represent goodness in heroics is only by negating some other fact.

In fact, there are entire schools that create these mental stories of how something in our life is not a part of the global good. Something we have some natural aversion to. Take that and say that we are still alive only because of some gracefulness and that anything that does not reach our standards of comfort must have been null, or unreal.

People in ancient times as well could not accept things as they are and created dreamy goodness feeling by attributing unrealism presenting the existence clause.

187

SELF ABNEGATION

What happens when we do not accept things as they are is not catastrophic. It is just how you may want to phrase it or word it. Our world is full of good and bad. We can start our own school of thought by being not accepting things that cause us difficulty.

There is an existence platform for everything and we are not doing fundamental research trying to find solutions to great big problems in life but spending our time in a qualitative way. What does one get by accepting that discomfort exists.

Practically we want to forget all the displeasure and start fresh. Probably the idea of using understandable theory that we can live through and talk about incorporates that we wish to talk only on these subjects and not about realism.

There are schools and people that evolve with the tacit understanding that human behavior and human stereotypes are far too disparate. There are people that do all sorts of things and have a propensity for what can be unnatural for us.

Trying to characterize ourselves in the wide spectrum of all sorts of things and people gives us a chance to describe ourselves as normal. There is always a set of people that go about their own way just not being extraordinary or compete with things that they cannot do.

There normal people liberate religion from war. They present stories saying that without a debate on the absolute world of perfection, we will just avoid a few things in life and discuss the topics devoid of discomfort or difficulty.

People create good stories of the nature of nonexistence of evil. It is probably one of the favorite religious sentiment to associate meditative quietness to something uncomplicated. We can create whatever story that we like and believe in what we want to believe.

If this question is ever asked in our civilization that what is a good way to deal with our life in this civilization. Are we better thinking and accepting things with qualitative good and bad and attempt to find life solutions with total accuracy and philosophical conclusion that is available to only the extraordinarily good or intelligent people. Or can we just say that self abnegation that takes the basic premise of constructing our story with a sense of success.

I will say it depends on how successful we are in creating a good quantity of story. Quantity of goodness and success really matters. If we are successful to have our time filled with even surreal stories but keeping the tacit understanding of over simplifying it would be as good as a solution. The point of difference in being realistic or not is called length.

188

COMMUNICATIONS

I do not know what can be perceived of negation. Problem solving in an attitude is a good parallel to duality. We need to understand how we solve problems and find solutions. If everything was as straight forward, we would know how to number our solutions as well.

One solution as a possibility is not philosophy. It starts when you have two solutions not because it is correct. It just means that we know what we are surrounded with. Most of the problems in our world are communicated. That means the solution for in general what is understood in the regime of communication is subject to those dynamics.

Once we know that the dynamic is coming from the framework of communication we know that there is no straight forward way to revel in purist form of problem solving. It is quite phenomenal to research on some human propensities like problem solving or composing or even being alone are intelligent pursuits.

During one of these intelligent pursuits we know how we can find what is generic format of being a part of communication centered civilization. The world and people in our region are communication centric. What needs to be understood is how to portion our vestitude.

Suppose we have one shot at it. That means whatever we do we know that we can only be pushing our limits and intelligences and give our best to only one thing. Then it is fairly a good point to defocus and dilute our vehemence and effort to of doing somethings in our communicating domain of things.

In communication pretty much, the success is mental. You might find an animal under study being as successful in our world as one that does not use discretion to vest intelligence and solve things and find communications as being the basis of things.

I wish I could say that sequential forms have negation built into it. Because what ever in our world or life is communication based, there are only two dynamics to the story. One thing is to put things in a sequence and the other is to use parallelism to create the required tangibility.

We have to negate our great big conclusions from our human interaction with the metaphysical level as just another place of occupation by not so deserving people. The moment we preclude people of intelligent nature not to participate in all that is known is called one of the most fundamental part of our religion. It is called revelation.

We need to understand that we are not in a competitive story as being communicated also. If you are being communicated with it is as easy as negating the communication because communication does not promise quality.

189

EGO AND IMPOSED STORY

Finding ourselves as a part of this civilization just as another thing that is talking around or being talked with is all there is to create the stillness. Now let us try to understand that communication systems don't provide solutions. What is consisted in a communication system is just a fair bit of what it takes to be in the neutral territory.

The very fact that anybody can talk, or everybody is human kind of clauses need certain inconclusive directions. Inconclusive part of our story is a characteristic on things like time. Therefore, we can say that time does not constitute negation.

The more we adhere to our life the better we find that doing things one after the other is ritualistic. It is only unsuccessful that has parallelism and needs to be propped.

We do not get anything out of doing something as prescribed as it just occupied space and time. Why have been these humans been successful is that they have eaten a hundred years of time and are very competitive with common mediocrity and do not publish failure.

Mediocrity is where the ritual is as well. The most important part of our religion is to be able to do something or the other easily. When we get a chance, we need to see how simplicity or being easy consists mirror.

Self is easy and simple. It is a form of happiness or joy. But the only thing is that it is not competitive. We will get somewhere else when we try to make things difficult and compare it to find the easy parts as a mirror or self.

There needs to be a lot of research that needs to be dome to w not to emulate self with our mental aptitude for easy things. In our modern civilization we can find live artefacts that will not survive a mirror. Why did religious leaders stop intruding into lives with all sorts of mirrors? Is there a scientific incentive to not reveal the actuality?

What are all the things that ire in competition and what is actually driving our civilization. We cannot say that we neither want to focus on solution nor we will stop trying to make things as simple but irreligious. We need to stop chasing things as the destined people for doing the job is not quite as intuitive.

We need to develop secret initiatives that focus on the actual values of self and solution. We have to develop new social paradigms as we cannot undo things that have been input into our systems by ineptitude from unknown parts of the world. We have to experiment being honest where it matters and be not squandering and getting the incentive.

190

USE OF DREAMS

What is the difference between communication and research. People are redundant in the light of a dream. Dream constitutes nothing but a disperse of effort. What do we spend our time chasing or doing or even understanding is arbitrary in the definitional format? What defines a dream is more likely to represent civilization because we do not know where the momentum is coming from.

We can either commit to the fact that if we use dream to communicate a story it is definitely inundated in a form of correctness. Why would a dream as a way of communicating is more tangible than writing an essay or even speaking?

It is a question of vested interest. There is quite a lot that gets done to understand life while we are in it. So, the inundated part of the dream includes the way we exist in something. It is obvious that we are being into something in life is a parallel to we are being inundated in a dream as well.

There is quite a lot of research that does not constitute human expression. So, dreams unlike communications do not constitute a way of expression. Dream is by far the farthest object to poetry. What is objective in a dream is that it runs a parallel to life.

There must have been quite a lot of similarity in our existence with all the things we do in our life and the story that is contained in a dream. Dream does include personage but most often it is defined as being stationary.

There is no interpretation as I know of the personage contained in a dream. Dream constitute the moving part of our life. We all move here and there, and we move things and thoughts as well until something is settled or set up the way we want.

Dream is a disperse of artefacts that take a form and shape of life like activity. Dreams are definitely not as much story oriented. They are just what they are containing a form of human effort. Sometimes the initial parts of our human story start with a dream.

Why do people use dreams to begin something? It is because the confidence it takes to understand life or even a certain part of nature is fundamentally rooted in metaphysical. We attempt to interpret nature and initiate a nature study for example and take the understanding to a metaphysical nature of our opinion or thought on a particular subject.

All the matter in our life in not although set up in metaphysical but definitely the process of understanding is represented in metaphysical and the dream related to a set of activities done as a part of research contains the subtle part of the entire project. We need to see all the beginnings that are built and transmitted in dream. A good dream is a good starting point of something.

191

SOCIAL SENTIMENT

Social sentiment is what contains the stability required to put something across. Most often what our social structure consists is a volume of data we generate in our research.

A good format of working research has it's beginning in a dream and conclusion in society. We are taking various initiatives to understand things of nature or psychology. We do not particularly fail in our attempts, but we do stop sometimes.

What happens when we stop in study is that there is an implicit sense of requirement for conclusion and social is the place to conclude.

Explicit and implicit failure is a part of any study. Social does not persuade or create the need that we have to study things. As complicated as things are the entirety of all that we use as a part of our psychology in a particular study must be represented in social.

Why is it not explicit that social sentiment is the repository for failures?

Successful studies take a form of being our self or personal artefacts and failure takes the shape of the volume of all that society holds.

What happens during a study is an interaction of ourselves with the metaphysical.

We interpret the metaphysical existence to contain what we research. All is not an interpretation of the existence. Due to the complex nature we sometimes fail. The only thing that remains uninterpretable or un attempted is mostly social.

Our society holds quite a lot of still artefacts. It has a tendency not to judge things as human individual does. There is always flow of volumes of information between a person and social structure.

Schools of thought remain in seclusion in metaphysical interaction of our study and when we discontinue something we inherently interact with social. It is not clear how social structure is different from metaphysical.

The need for metaphysics and social sentiment is the format of human. We continue to grow alongside this story with the great complexity. Interaction of human with these sources needs to be described with all the subtle and beautiful things that there are in our existence. We need to characterize our surroundings with effort.

192

MANAGEMENT

Realism is the most difficult part of our dictionary. The reason in government or management. We as social human beings get exposed to either one of them. What exactly is happening that makes our life in the reflection of government or management so very obscure.

Our life is a series of events. As with anything else our life gets created in one way or the other understandable to us. The problem is verification of life. Life like characterization and even initiative to verify something in our life is the primary motive of any program.

So essentially government is a sensory program that take our life into surrealism just so that we can call our life verifiable.

What exactly happens is that our life as it is, is sensitive to creation. There is one end where we create our life as we want. There are all sorts of influences from all over the place. The social initiative is to disperse our life or events in our lives at the very source or creation.

Once we all settle to the realism that we influence each other by creating events in our lives we will know what we have at hand. Pure forma of life is not associated with our likes and dislikes. Life is not in its nascent form characterized. This question less form of life goes on with the only notion of calling it a name.

We do not know what life is because it exists around us silently only susceptible to be named as something and does not interact in any other manner with our intellect. With the given form of uninteractive form of life that we have been given into we develop a social sentiment.

We develop social emotions of likes and dislikes and most importantly similarity. With our social life around us we develop a lot of initiatives. We create a life likeness and hold it with our hand. We begin to manipulate this life like format using our emotion.

We begin to experience that we can affect, or influence life based on our intellectual experience. While life goes on we develop these time consuming characterizations such as events. Events also have life in them, but they are just figments of our imagination something we do to ourselves out of some requirement to have a social response.

As a result, the quieter form of our life is not only not understood but it is clouded with this other artefact of how we fill our lives with the capability to influence our life with a certain will. This is the core of the conflict is that what is this life like character that consumes time and our will.

We need to know that a lot of intellectual definition in within our intellect. We can only be cyclical.

193

MEDIA

With all the notions of social relevance we have we do interact with each other in more than one way. The understanding of putting will into our life is central to the theme. We have a sense of will because of emotion or our propensity in what we want.

Likes and dislikes become an integral part of our life and we go on living our lives experiencing this format of life where we have a certain personage trying to manipulate life. Some people call it the social being while some call it the flavor of life.

It is just not possible to understand life or interact with it. We just keep wielding what we create that runs a parallel. We need to call them event creation than calling it life.

We all develop a certain instinct when we get into these event managements. Social life is just so inundated with events that we can almost lose all of the life to just wielding it.

What we have almost in entirety is just a reflection. We almost make it impossible to have anything other than what we can understand as created. I fail to understand this paradigm and why is it popular. The natural characterization and selection almost become a study instead of being a part of our life.

Natural selection needs to be researched. We either need to publish that we live a manipulative reflectance of instead of nature. We need to study more extensively the otherwise condition by trying to manipulate it completely as we will never get natural enough to liberate ourselves.

Our manipulated artefact of reflectance of life becomes even more enjoyable trying to create a story. I believe that media and movies are not stand alone creations in our society. They form at very fundamental levels and need to be treated as by products than thinking how to treat it with a sense of disconnect.

We develop so many instincts of denial when we begin to profess how natural we are. We believe that media and movies are the product of our creation that calling our lives in their actuality as a manipulated and created artefact.

So, in general we have another paradigm of some attempt to represent life like thing in media or movies. We qualify our lives using media or movies as a reference. We will just have no semblance to nature than saying we have an architecture where we qualify one with the other. Anyway, we can incorporate respect into our existence by using relativism.

We can create realism that is necessary tailored to our situation using intellectual metric.

194

STORY OF SIMPLICITY

Simplicity is nothing but the opposite of complexity. Our life is very complex. The complexity of our life is evident from what all is justified in its presence in our life. We deserve mostly the format and nature of life as it is.

It is a good research topic to understand in which schools is this stream of thought encouraged. We cannot underestimate the nature of socialistic simplicity. These people took the complex nature of our life and psychology and created informal solutions.

Life and its value can only be judged from its original form. What could have been the advantage when some of the socialist thought attempted to liberate the discernible part of our existence and said that lets us over simplify our life to the point of isolating a couple of aspects of our life and treat the objectivity and disperse these points of interest as common goal.

The over simplification from these regions of the world is another topic of research. Now the question is what the definition of simplicity is. Is it just taking a problem and finding the commonality, deleting it from the volume and focusing on the residue.

Simplicity is a psychological conclusion of solving something complex in its entirety and not just an over simplified un common parts of subjects. What typically happens in these schools of thought they attempt to age people to take the thought process of considering life and holding the complexity in hand for as long as it takes for the mind to stabilize.

Mind needs to focus on the entire picture of what interests us as the incentive or even motivation. Maybe we all have a natural instinct to solve something all its original form. We have to consider our human stereotype on reflection of the problem we attempt.

Once we pitch our self in its entire psychological perspective to live with the problem then we can understand how we interact with the metaphysical. Interacting with the metaphysical with our mind poised to solve life is central to the theme.

This is the origin of simplistic forms of mental composition that some of the great people in the history hold. They took the entire complexity and were able to answer the question of life. It led them to the light of knowledge and were able to describe it in poetry and science.

We need to get used to the simplicity of solving complex problems and get into the stream of considering the life related topics with a degree of complexity and give it the appropriate amount of the portion of effort it takes, or we will just be uttering words and not the solution to the problems that may have been just present to take us to the beauty. There is not much that can be said in the intent of nature than presenting life to us in a disparate form.

195

SCHOOLS

Various schools of thought exist with a promise of providing the time it takes to solve our life and contribute to the things we like. The idea of having a school of thought is that it is not a sequential event that some people look for.

People are thinking how to understand life and contribute to the beauty of this world. There are certain artefacts that are attractive to these people. Philosophy, science, research and topics of mind are of interest. People have realized that special form of attention needs to be invested to understand the complexity of our lives.

Life is a beautiful, sensitive and a complex form of parallelism that is present everywhere. Preliminary scopes into study often reveal failures to explain and handle things of beauty. The disperse of people and what they do is not anything other than reflecting he popular format of government freedom.

Why can't problems be solved in governance itself. Because there is only one nature of complexity when it comes to life and not two. The existing complexity is not unfortunately the simplicity to throw an artefact into society and calling it popular.

It is good that the generic form of disperse of anything social is quite low level as compared to the existing forms of attempts to study anything for that matter. There is not a school that has been efforting bringing divine knowledge to people.

Social is not the place to find either the time or the motivation to consider problems of nature and beauty. People that realized this considered life as an individual prerogative and understood that there exist people with motivation to think on the lines of complex patterns.

They took the initiatives to establish well organized places where research is conducted. They opened schools of thought not only for themselves but also the nature of study that philosophy constitutes.

Nature of philosophy as some people attempt in their life is not a competitive form of some output that government chooses to monitor for the greater good of the society and the redundant forms of people and their emotion.

I believe that there exists a high form of existence that controls schools of thought and helps people that are not into the business of philosophy with enough incentive or opportunity. It is quite interesting what form does social takes if we seclude schools of thought. The remaining must have something to do with the nature of revolutions in the history and all the effort that leads to leadership and family. Hope this will be useful.

196

ESTABLISHMENT

At this stand point in our time our civilization is individualistic. It means that for some natural reasons the incentives are not clear and the disperses of sentiment is free. The amount of propaganda is sky high.

Individual propensities take time to flourish. There is time for everything. The reason to believe that in the time to come there will be a clear difference in individuals. There will be either two or three classes in our human race.

Classification of human beings has been a long time objective of various establishments. Theoretical classifications have evolved in religion on either this basis or that. In early 20th century there has been an unprecedented amount of intellectual call.

It is not usual for human beings to call upon a sensitive topic as respecting intellectuals as is. But it happened and there was one initiative after the other trying to put intelligent people in place.

This was the tacit establishment that followed similar pattern for the fifty years to come. By the mid of 20th century there were well recorded scientific and social achievements. The accomplishment in these fifty years consumed pretty much everything that we have in a good way. Although there were wars and opportunism, people had time not to fall for psychological games that are usual to our native propensity.

Such an establishment of human talent in the first half of 20th century outlined certain research outcome. Although as with any intellectual exercise, the entire result of this establishment is not clear but definitely the avenues for science and social sentiment including politics, government, and economy were well understood and put into a predictive paradigm

The only thing left out to have original research composition is research in ancient history. Everything else was more than understood. Therefore, we are in a paradigm that has been well understood and characterized for quite a long time and carved into our recent history.

What we have now is just following what has been studied and metering the various amounts of research outcome into economic paradigm. So most of the research reached an equilibrium with economic form. The next thing is to liberate the human from the inside to find himself.

This is one more reason that religion has never been more popular than ever before. People find themselves to distinguish oneself from the other in various number of ways. Everything else is given. It will be a great to see what this selection process is going to achieve in the human race and what is to be proliferated. There is only one way individual relevance can be felt. Rest of the human drama or human story does not consume effort. And what consumes effort is true.

197

HUMAN

In recent history people have started a lot of initiatives. Mostly the pseudo culture that has evolved to represent one self in the relevant platform in economic system resulted in most of the redundant human tendencies to be called into relevance.

Redundant human talent that seemed a little more random seemed intelligent to people in some areas and experiments are being conducted to try a different human prototype that can be more successful in our current regime whatever it may be. Although there are not a lot of combinations to human character that leads to success we have interfered in every segment.

The reason why there is wayward incentive is very much deep rooted beyond the imagination of the person that is benefiting from the randomness of human characterization that is going to create a ripple and create the next game out of randomness.

This randomness of the game of characterizations and incentives essentially creates some ways of representing and communicating our place in the society. People have been asked to describe what they see or fell in the given imposed framework of things and establishments.

Every human in this reflection of unknown and randomness has been feeling quite a lot of things in quite a lot of fanciful ways and being asked for clearly explaining one's self in more than one number of places has become a fashion.

The reason why we are asked to express ourselves is still not clear as there is not much research that we have done on our own. Anyway, we began to do things half of our time and got into the slow habit of explaining ourselves and our situation to people around in all possible ways. Some people have made an entertaining business out of explaining one's self.

People have gone as far to describe this pseudo habit as the story of life. The correct language positioning us where we are is what is your story. As if we all have something matter full to have an effect on the future.

It is quite sarcastic avocation we have evolved into that we call what we live in not from the goodness of the stability that we owe to our family but dilute it to defining our perspective as unique as calling it one's story. Having described it well is not much of relevance than giving into pseudo art that perceives people and lives in a casual and nonchalant way of the art that has been thoughtful of the sensitive side of the story.

In modern society incentive is driven by how we define our position in the human story and how we characterize ourselves and be aware of what sentiment we are a part of. Some people are more successful but that does not mean that mindless avocation do create natural ways of differences.

198

INCENTIVES

We have a reason to believe that there is insolvability associated with government. The point to intellectual realization and exercise is to liberate. And let us say that people in early 20th century were successfully able to create this liberation.

The essence of liberation is to put into light something. We do not know what it is to feel. The aftermath of the events in first half of the 20th century stood in competition with the generic civilization.

The common man with his usual story has been as competitive with government and a certain form of religious dogma on his side. It is always the most intelligent to hold a position to have negated something. So, let us assume for this exercise that the common man and his consortium stood in realism of negating what happened in the research of the early 20th century.

Although it is as generic in nature to hope our religion or government to negate establishment and research of a very high intellectual level. People needed to feel important negating something intelligent. And this social sentiment took off without any obstruction.

So, I hold the position to think that the current circumstances and the present emotion in our civilization is devoid of respect to his levels of intellectuality. Not only that, we do have a certain incentive to deride the most intelligent events in our history.

Whatever it is the story of the common man and his incentive will stand and proliferate for a very long time. The longevity of these incentivized existences has always been in question. The point is we do not know for how long the current scheme of incentives will go on in our civilization. For definitely a very long time and it is worthwhile to portion a certain part of our energy towards the current establishment and see how we can do our study in this realm.

The actual original research can be said to have opposite incentives as we have now. I do not know of any school of thought that has been anti establishment and dispute the levels of incentive to negate and deride standalone platforms.

Still there are parts of our religion that provide the incentive to continue to do original research. How did religion ever stand derision is not clear. May be people of humanitarian cause are way too bust with their machinations.

The point is it is undeniable that in our present culture it is only natural to find the most intelligent people and the most intelligent research to be centered in religion. It is interesting to see what the primary definition of the negatable matter of our society is as proposed in religion. Surely there exists a lot of similarity between the current school of thought and Vedic negations constituted Neti Neti.

199

ADHERENCE

Intellectual part of the religion has to be researched. It is as good as the scientific research that changed the dimension of our civilization. The amount of originality and intelligence that exists in the religious study is unprecedented.

Religious study has been able to establish the undeniable connection to the formats of ancient cultures that hold the epitome of human psychology. Another research topic is to conduct a comparative study of the religious psychology for example as exhibited in Vedic scriptures to let's say the current format of the structure of religion in developed countries.

The basis of a successful economic theory is very similar to have an existential advantage that stands time. How did ever the psychological nature as readable in Vedic scriptures evidently show similarities with the religious policy as contained in the schools of thought in developed and successful countries.

It will be worthwhile to study the research for example on speculative philosophy from the western world. Anything to do with time is fundamentally adherential. We stick to time. Neti Neti. There is as fundamental and all pervasive in our life as has been naturally and historically. We must take our mind off the incentives and focus on research and psychological formats that have stood time.

I would like to research how the tone of religion adheres to time. It is a great opportunity to have adherential value in our research. This is what makes something comparable to realizable levels of human interaction with the metaphysical.

Soon there will be special schools of thought that proliferate anti incentive psychology. Some parts of religion will be liberated as a part of global initiate to study history. Surely there is a lot of time and culture that is vested in our history not to separate it and nurture things in a standalone format as the individuals of our past have been able to do it all by themselves.

The current civilization does not provide the necessary from to take an intellectual ride. Everything is fragmented and reasoned out in analysis.

What constitutes life and inundation of humans in time is in our history, but current state of affair is centered how as a team of social initiative can we distribute wealth.

We also need to research what are the religious good points that are covered in advanced economic policy of rich countries.

It will be evident that the uncompromising attitude that is necessary to stand time is within religion.

200

FAILURES

In general subjects that deal with conclusivity ore often only social. Social objectives alone contain a set of conclusivities. So, we can say that anything that is not a part of research or our understanding exists in social way ofn6 life.

No one researches on social. Social artefacts are so redundant that the matter contained in our society id almost ununderstandable. It is probably the way things are defined or the language in which the social structure is set up.

Social artefacts and sentiments are just a part of our life consuming a lot of our focus. There is not a school of thought that encourages research to be distant to society. Why is it important to be social if it does not contribute to our understanding?

Social sentiment has always had the promise to contain the stability the is required in a natural or a biological set up.

I am sure the certain fundamental concepts of nature and biology run a parallel to social sentiment. Social sentiment is like an emotion that is present to take care of failure. When a certain research or a study fails it takes a form of looking for conclusion.

So, we just dump the entire study along with the failure in social sentiment and hope that the stability would be able to take the redundant volume that constitutes a failed attempt in psychology or science.

Religion is a reserved form of social; sentiment also contributing to stability in the light of failed initiatives. Why we fail in our study and attempts of understanding is not clear. Some people may believe that there is an unresolved conflict that comes from social sentiment that makes us lose control of our study.

Every human has his own initiative. Social does not promote or dissuade our attempts to understand something. Social sentiment often contains certain formats that are similar to human psychology when it is involved in a study for example.

And there is quite a lot that is masked from making a person feel more responsible that just being as responsible as one is naturally. That is the drawback of the social sentiment is that although it is useful in failures it does not provide the momentum it takes to do something.

We can experiment by creating a beginning in a dream and ending in social volume and definitely spend a good amount of time just doing something. Not everything is as full of acceptance as social.

www.ingramcontent.com/pod-product-compliance
Lightning Source LLC
La Vergne TN
LVHW050535160826
845677LV00011B/2048

* 9 7 9 8 8 9 0 2 6 0 1 5 4 *